SARASVATI RIVER AND THE VEDIC CIVILIZATION

Sarasvati River and the Vedic Civilization

History, science and politics

N.S. RAJARAM

ADITYA PRAKASHAN
New Delhi

(nsrajaram@vsnl.com)

F2 'RAJATHA MANOR'
Patalamma Temple Road, Southend Circle
Basvanagudi, BANGALORE — 560 004
Tel: 080 – 2657 9985

First published, 2006

ISBN 81-7742-066-6

Published by Aditya Prakashan, F-14/65, Model Town II, Delhi – 110 009.
email: aditya@bibliaimpex.com

Printed at Rajkamal Electric Press, Delhi – 110 033.

To two pioneers:

V.S. Wakankar
and
N. Jha

Contents

Foreword

What textbooks today describe as the facts of ancient history in regard to India unfortunately are little more than speculation. They may tell us more about the cultural prejudices of the people writing history than about the ancients themselves. Modern Western accounts of ancient India are not nearly as scientific as they present themselves. Western materialistic civilization has not always had the depth to understand the development of a spiritual culture like that of India. It also suffered from an ethnocentric approach that has generally given little credit to civilizations outside its sphere of influence, like those of India, China or the (pre-Columbian) Americas.

Ancient history of course is not an objective science that allows for easy verification. It has some solid evidence to build on, with various ruins and artifacts, but these are limited, often found by chance, and subject to various, even contradictory interpretations. Other tools of historical interpretation are more subjective and very difficult to verify. The so-called linguistic evidence—the main tool used to interpret the ancient history of India—is little more than guesswork. It uses language fragments from different periods and cultures to try to reconstruct what prehistoric languages were and through that determine the migration of peoples. It is rooted not in one but several assumptions: that modern scholars with a different mentality and in a radically different cultural context can put together ancient languages from mere fragments [often from a much later period], and then determine the nature of the cultures that produced them and the directions they moved during prehistoric eras requires a great leap of faith and can hardly be called anything factual.[1]

---

[1]It in fact goes even further. So-called 'historical linguistics' attempts to reconstruct long vanished languages (which may or may not have existed) by working backwards from such fragments. These reconstructions, called 'proto-languages', are then used to draw conclusions about the supposed speakers of these languages. The conclusions are then presented as historical possibilities often without informing readers that neither the proto-language nor its speakers may have ever existed. Quantitave tests have brought the whole of Indo-European linguistics into question. (N.S.R.)

Determining the ancient history of a vast subcontinent is a very complex matter that can easily lend itself to distortion. Yet, if we look at the history of ancient India, as textbooks portray it, it is a highly simplistic matter of an outside invasion of primitive tribes from Central Asia, the so-called Aryans, even though there is no archaeological evidence for any Aryan invasion into India.[2] Rather than proving the invasion, it assumes the invasion to be true and then molds the factual data to fit it, even if the data has to be altered in order to do so.

History is also a political issue. Many political and religious points can be scored through promoting historical interpretations that give credence to particular cultural values or call others into question. History can have immense propaganda value. To discredit a culture's own idea of its history can help undermine it for purposes of political or religious domination. Each religious and political ideology, not surprisingly, has written history in its own image, generally by people promoting European, communist, capitalist, Christian and Islamic viewpoints and denigrating any traditional Hindu views. Even good scholars can fall prey to such motivations, which are deeply rooted in the cultural psyche.

Not surprisingly, the history of India as portrayed in modern textbooks dominated by Western thinking is an embarrassment to Hindus that causes them to distrust their ancestors. It shows not a noble indigenous people—which is the traditional Vedic view—but nomads, invaders, and barbarian hordes weaving a tale of superstition, destruction and deception—a view that non-Hindu groups can easily use for their own benefit. If this were a scientifically proved fact, one would have to live with it, but the facts actually are quite contrary.

Fortunately today, there is a revolution happening in the historical interpretation of India. The Aryan invasion model is crumbling like a house of cards. The Vedic view of ancient India is being re-vindicated, not by wild speculation, but the most solid evidence and combination of disciplines.

The new re-examination of ancient India proceeds by an interdisciplinary approach. Archaeological evidence in terms of cities, artifacts, agriculture and metallurgy is combined with studies of ancient river systems, which differ significantly from those of the present day.

---

[2]It is now contradicted by genetic evidence. See *Out of Eden* by Stephen Oppenheimer in the Bibliography.

These in turn can be correlated to Vedic literature, science and astronomy, which has hitherto been ignored or scaled down according to the invasion assumption. The resulting data can be cross-referenced with that from nearby cultures like Egypt and Babylonia. The combined data reveals the Vedic Civilization within India going back to prehistoric times as the main culture of the region.

Navaratna Rajaram is one of the foremost scholars of this new view of ancient India. He has produced several books and numerous articles that cover all facets of the issues involved. *Sarasvati River and the Vedic Civilization* summarizes most of this data and places it in a clear perspective. Rajaram has created the most complete reconstruction of ancient Indian history to date, giving precise dates for all the important events and all the different strata of Vedic literature. His interpretation gives credence to the ancient Hindu idea that the Mahabharata War and the time of Sri Krishna occurred around 3100 BC and provides the most thorough justification so far for this date.

However, Rajaram is not arguing from a point of faith. He is speaking as a scientist and goes back to factual data of all types to support his claim. He also exposes religious and political preconceptions that may distort historical data. Even if one does not accept all of his conclusions, we must be prepared to revise the whole history of the world and take a new look at what human beings are supposed to be.

Perhaps the key evidence is the ancient course of the Sarasvati River, which once flowed from the Ambala hills to the Rann of Kachch. The river was the greatest river in India before 7000 BC, after which it began to decline. It was fed by the melting glaciers at the end of the Ice Age and gradually declined along with them. The end of the great Harappan age occurred around 2000 BC along with the final drying up of the Sarasvati as a perennial stream in the north. The course of the Sarasvati described in Vedic literature relates not only to its Harappan but also its pre-Harappan flow going back to the time when the Sarasvati flowed to the sea as the greatest river in India, which is how the great river is lauded in the Vedas.

There were two main regions of the ancient Sarasvati. First was its upper region or doab wherein it took on various smaller streams to become a great river. Such an area with many converging streams (like the modern Punjab) is quite favorable for agriculture, cities and the development of civilization. This was the region between the Sutlej and the Yamuna, which both previously flowed into the Sarasvati system, Sutlej then flowing south and east, and Yamuna south and west of their present courses. The central part of the Sarasvati was the Kurukshetra, the Divine Land of the Brahmins between the Sarasvati and the Drishadvati, where Manu, the first Vedic king and lawgiver was said to have established his domain.

Second was the lower region or the delta of the Sarasvati. The Sarasvati flowed primarily into the Rann of Kachch, but a branch of it flowed south and east into the Gulf of Khambhat, picking up the smaller rivers of Gujarat along the way. The older flow the Sarasvati connected to the Luni River. The Sarasvati delta thus included the Rann of Kachch, the Kathiawar Peninsula and the Gulf of Khambhat. It connected closely to the Indus delta to the West and the mouths of the Mahi, Narmada and Tapti rivers that also flow into the Gulf of Khambhat, making a broad coastal riverine region quite favorable for the development of populations and for maritime trade and travel (though not as favorable for the preservation of ruins, which were subject to changing coastlines and the build up of silt in the delta regions).

Not surprisingly these are the two most important regions both in the Vedic literature and in Harappan ruins. The importance of Kurukshetra in the late Vedic literature is well known. Many Harappan sites are located in this region as well. Both southern Vedic holy sites, like Dwaraka (Kushasthali) and Somnath on the Kathiawar peninsula, are also explained by this, as are the great Harappan seaports like Lothal (in the Kathiawar peninsula) and Dholavira (in Kachch).

The first of the places of pilgrimage for the Sarasvati River in the *Mahabharata* is the site of Somnath (Prabhas) on the Kathiawar peninsula in Gujarat. The last two are the Sarasvati's origin at Plaksha Prasravarana and the Kurukshetra itself, which were not far away.[3] The Somnath site makes sense only if one considers the eastward branch of the Sarasvati that flowed into the Gulf of Khambhat. The famous Harappan port of Lothal would thereby have been on an old branch of the Sarasvati. The connection between Gujarat and eastern Punjab as Harappan regions becomes obvious: they are the doab and the delta of the Sarasvati.

We note in Vedic literature many ancient figures like Sharyata, the son of Manu, and Bhrigu and rishis like Chyavana and Shukra are associated

---

[3]Plaksha Prasravana, the birthplace of the Sarasvati was known also as Plaksagra. The latter word is found on at least one of the deciphered Indus seals. So is Dvaravati as Dwaraka was also known.

with Gujarat, while Ila, Manu's daughter and Angirasa rishis were associated with the Sarasvati-Drishadvati region (doab). *The upper Sarasvati was the land of the Purus and the Bharatas in the Vedic literature; the lower Sarasvati was the land of the Yadus.* Purus and Yadus were the dominant peoples in the Vedic literature to the time of Krishna, with the Kauravas and the Pandavas belonging to the Puru line and Krishna to the Yadu line. Now this fits in perfectly with the knowledge of the rivers of the region. The Vedic people are placed by the sea in Gujarat at the beginning of the Vedic period, which goes far to explain the strong oceanic symbolism in the *Rigveda,* the oldest of the Vedas.

Similarly perhaps the key for determining the time of Krishna is determining when the Sarasvati existed as described in the *Mahabharata.* Harappan sites have been found only in the upper course of the Sarasvati. They don't appear to go beyond Ramiyar Khan in Pakistan. If this is the case, then it would appear that even in the Harappan era the Sarasvati did not flow all the way to the sea. The places where Harappan sites come to an end on the Sarasvati may mark the *Vinashana* of the late Vedic literature, the place where the Sarasvati was said to have dried up in the desert. Like the Harappan sites, *Vinashana* was near the Panchanada or five-river Punjab region in North India. It is said to be forty-four days horse ride from the origin of the river above Kurukshetra near Ambala. I am not certain what a day's horse ride could be, but the total distance is only about five hundred miles on the map, which would not be illogical for forty days of horse riding.[4] This means there is evidence to suggest that the Sarasvati as portrayed in the *Mahabharata* is similar to the Sarasvati as it existed during the Harappan era (c. 3100–1900 BC). As the *Mahabharata* mentions forests and lakes along the course of the Sarasvati, it does not appear to relate to the river as it occurred after 1900 BC, when it ceased to be a perennial stream.

However, whether the *Mahabharata* dates from 3000 BC or somewhat later, the Vedic nature of ancient Indian civilization would not change. This is proved by the Vedic knowledge of the course of the Sarasvati as it

---

[4]About twelve to fifteen miles a day for comfortable travel with a loaded packhorse and an entourage. A relay of horses with well equipped relay stations could of course cover a great deal more ground, but this requires massive logistic support. So five hundred miles in forty-four days of leisurely travel including sight seeing is perfectly reasonable as I can vouch from personal experience. Also, Balarama is said to have cut short his journey when he heard of the war and returned in haste. (N.S.R.)

was in both Harappan and pre-Harappan eras. (This is discussed in the Appendix on the Date of the Mahabharata War.)

Sarasvati River and the Vedic Civilization examines these and other important issues in a succinct and lucid style and lays before the reader an important new approach to ancient India. It is important that this information is disseminated on as wide a basis as possible so that prevailing misconceptions can be corrected and the true history of India can be revealed. The book is a good introduction to the study of ancient India in a deeper light.

DAVID FRAWLEY
(VAMADEVA SHASTRI)

Preface

Science in the service of history

In this modest volume, what I have attempted is an easy to follow summary of some important findings of the last four decades that have a bearing on the civilization of Vedic India. Taken individually any one of them may seem minor, but their cumulative impact is monumental. They force a fundamental reorientation in our thinking by drawing attention to South India (Peninsular India) and Southeast Asia as possible major contributors to the Vedic civilization from the earliest times. Judging by recent discoveris in archaeology and natural history—including genetics—this shift of focus from the west and northwest to south and east is likely to be the next major development in Indian historiography. Anyone familiar with history books in use today can see this is a radical departure indeed. In doing this, I have also moved away from the battle of polemics relating to the various invasion/migration theories and taken what I hope are steps towards reconstructing history on rational grounds and on scientific principles.

I have called the book *Sarasvati River and the Vedic Civilization.* This to me seems entirely natural. The discovery of the lost river Sarasvati led to the rediscovery of our Vedic past. It highlights also the two major discoveries that came to light in the final decade of the last century: the Vedic river Sarasvati and the identification of the Harappan civilization as the Vedic-Sarasvati civilization. The latter culminated in Jha's proposed decipherment of the Indus script, in which I too had a part.

These two themes—the Sarasvati River and the Vedic-Harappan identity—form the core of the book. They take us beyond refuting prevailing theories like the Aryan invasion and offer a constructive alternative. But they are not the whole story. Science now tells us that there existed a primordial civilization flourishing by the Sarasvati River going back to 4000 BC if not a good deal earlier. The *Rigveda* is a remnant of that hoary age. Whether there existed an even earlier civilization of which the *Rigveda* was a part—or from which the Vedic civilization sprang—is a question we must be prepared to ask. I have just touched on it here, but hope to address it more fully in the future.[1]

This book is also the story of the search leading to the rediscovery of our ancient roots. We call this the Vedic Civilization, though this represents only the culmination of what must have been a long journey. It is also the story of the decline and fall of a theology of false doctrines created by colonial politicians and other interested parties to serve their own interests. It is this theology that is still being taught as 'history' in Indian schools and colleges. The present book was written partly to correct the picture. It refutes unfounded theories based on evidence. It goes beyond refutation by providing an alternative.

The process by which a false, scientifically discredited version happened to gain respectability as 'Indology' (and now Indo-European studies) is an integral part of Indian historiography. I have therefore found it useful to discuss its background in some detail. It is necessary to learn from past mistakes so we don't keep repeating them.

With this in view, I have added Supplement I, which summarizes in one place the scientific, the historical and the political background to the Aryan invasion theory, which has dominated discourse for well over a century. I hope the reader will see that the debate today, or what is left of it, is entirely political in which the advocates of the Aryan invasion have little to add beyond verbal semantics and negation of evidence.

For these reasons I have taken an uncompromising stand on the issue of Western inspired Indology: I see Indology as a 'period discipline' like eugenics (race science) and colonial anthropological theories that were created mainly to give a veneer of respectability to political and religious motives. I see it as having two sides—racial and political. The two became intermixed as in the case of German Nationalism, but continues today in the guise of Indo-European Studies. Though racism is no longer academically respectable, the same ideas, often with similar conclusions continue to be promoted in the guise of linguistics and anthropology. This has now acquired new life, and new patronage, in the guise of genetics—supposedly as the result of 'genome research'. I have found it worthwhile to show its true colors and separate science from propaganda.

---

[1]I have made a beginning in several articles relating pre- and proto-Vedic civilizations to maritime cultures of coastal India and Southeast Asia during the last ice Age. This is supported by natural history and population genetics. I have touched on the latter briefly in the book.

The book does not claim to be the final word on ancient history. Our voyage of discovery has only begun. It is not even entirely objective, for I have been too close to the events as well as to some of the key personalities whose work has made the present book possible. In any event, I doubt if such a thing as 'objective history' can ever exist. But I have no hesitation in asserting that the account given here is in much better agreement with empirical data than what is found in most history books today.

One of my goals in this book is to highlight the problems inherent in the current version of history and suggest alternatives based on science and the primary sources. If this provides room for thought, especially among the youth, I will be more than happy.

An emerging new field is the study of human genetics. Recent advances in the field have the potential to add significantly to our understanding of ancient history going back to the Ice Age. But what I have seen so far has tended to be naïve and at times motivated—with occasional attempts to revive discredited race theories in the guise of science. I have included some discussion of biological evidence, for it is bound to play an increasingly important role in the study of the ancient world. As I see it, the problem lies not so much with the biochemistry and the structure of genes, which are well understood, but a proper application of quantitative methods to human populations. I have occasionally touched on these topics but it needs many years of research before we can feel comfortable about genetic data and methods of analysis.

I feel that methods currently in use may not suffice and new ones may need to be created from fundamentals. Further, *we need to study human history as part of natural history*. This is an ambitious program. I have only touched on it in the present volume. I feel however that it is a new and important field that will attract the best talent in the coming decades.

Returning to the struggle for truth, what we are witnessing is in fact a rediscovery of the nearly lost roots of our Vedic past. Alien (and alienated) forces—both Indian and foreign—have done their best to erase all traces of its existence. But now, thanks to science and the dedication of many seekers, truth is finally coming to the fore. And naturally enough, for that reason, it is also a story of the struggle between truth seekers and false prophets—between light and darkness.

In the present volume, I have provided a summary of the following three major themes. First, an easy to follow but scientifically sound explanation of discoveries leading to the refutation of the model of history based on the notion of the Aryan invasion of India; this is based on, but not limited to, the Sarasvati River and the Vedic-Harappan connection. (This includes a popular acount of Jha's proposed decipherment of the Indus script.) Next, a brief summary of the colonial politics and missionary interests that led to the creation of this model. (For this reason, it is now being called the *colonial-missionary model.*) Finally, I give also a brief discussion of biological and ecological antecedents of history that call for a reorientation of our focus from the north-northwest to the south and the southeast. This I have only touched upon in the final chapter.

I have included also three supplementary chapters that present some facts about important topics and recent developments. They are related to topics discussed in the book, but may be read independently. Supplement I in particular contains important new information that is likely to have a major bearing on Indian history and historiography.

The present volume differs from most other books on the subject by going beyond refutation of the Aryan invasion and providing an alternative approach to reconstructing ancient history. (I have also touched on the possible westward diffusion of language and culture, based partly on Shrikant Talageri's Vedic-Puranic synthesis. This needs the support of hard data from science and archaeology, which one hopes will not be long in coming. A beginning has been made by geneticists Luigi Cavalli-Sforza and Stephen Oppenheimer in their recent research, which I have briefly touched on. Results so far indicate that *all* non-African peoples living in the world today are desended from South Asians.

In terms of chronology, the present volume departs from the accounts found in most history books on these two points: (1) identification of the Harappan civilization as Vedic; and (2) placing the *Rigveda* before the material civilization represented by Harappan archaeology. The history of the Sarasvati River provides the theme, for the history of the Sarasvati River is veritably the history of the Vedic Age.

If there is one message that I have tried to convey it is that science and the primary sources must take precedence over theory and beliefs. As Einstein once said: "A theory must not contradict empirical facts."

Acknowledgements

I am grateful to David Frawley (Vamadeva Shastri) for contributing his informative Foreword. I have benefited also from the suggestions of Swami Mukhyanandaji Maharaj of Belur Math, and his constant encouragement. I am particularly grateful to Natwar Jha and Birendra Kumar Jha for sharing with me their thoughts and discoveries relating to the Indus script. Natwar Jha has also shared with me his profound insights into the symbolism of Harappan iconography, which I have discussed extensively with David Frawley. I am grateful also the distinguished geologist, Dr. B.P. Radhakrishna, for his time and courtesy in the face of my many inquiries about the ecology of the Sarasvati River.

I am grateful also to Beluru Sudarshana for bringing out a preliminary version of the book, which proved widely popular. The present volume is a substantial revision of that book, especially with regard to the natural history section. My thanks also to S. Kalyanaraman of the Sarasvati River Foundation, Chennai, for his generous help with some of the source material, especially for making available to me the seal images in electronic form that are used here.

Finally, I am grateful to The Naimisha Research Foundation of Bangalore, and its friends for supporting the research leading to the book.

Makara Sankranti 2006

Oklahoma City, U.S.A.
Bangalore, India

1.

Introduction: Science and faith

Theology and the scientific method

Science is concerned with explaining nature by discovering its laws. Theology seeks to find support for a given belief. Science and theology therefore represent two diametrically opposite ways of looking at the world. The scientist, especially the empirical scientist, has to deal with the facts and evidence as he finds them in the real world. When there is a conflict between real-world data and his pet theory, the theory loses, no matter how beautiful its form or how eminent the scientist who created it. Suppose one has an elegant theory about the building of Egyptian pyramids, but it is found to contradict Newton's Law of Gravitation. Then the theory falls. In science, a single contradictory empirical fact is all it takes to overthrow an established theory. History of science is full of such examples. A single negative result coming out of the Michelson-Morley experiment was all it took to dethrone Newtonian physics—leading Einstein to create his Theory of Relativity. It was Einstein who said: "A theory must not contradict empirical facts."

A theologian on the other hand takes the opposite approach: a particular doctrine or a set of doctrines is held to be inviolate. Every new finding must support this doctrine failing which it is rejected as false. For example, when Galileo's discoveries about the solar system showed the sun to be at the center of our planetary system, it was rejected for being in conflict with Church dogma. Thus, in theology, truth is defined in terms of conformity with doctrine. Anyone who makes claims in conflict with the approved doctrine is called a heretic. Where science is based on freedom of thought, the basis of theology is dogma.

It is not merely religion that defines truth in terms of doctrines and dogmas—some political and social systems do so as well. For instance, in Stalinist Soviet Union, geneticists were branded as heretics and persecuted. Stalin's favorite Trofim Lysenko had acquired dictatorial control over biological research. He declared genetics to be an anti-Marxist capitalist plot. Using his influence with Stalin, he exiled several distinguished geneticists including the great N. Vavilov who died in a Siberian prison. This seriously set back Soviet agricultural research from which Russia has still not recovered. There is not much difference between Galileo's persecution by the Church, and Vavilov's persecution by the Stalinist Soviet Union.

Viewed in this light, Indian history as presented and taught in the past century and a half must also be regarded as a theology built around a central doctrine. This doctrine is: Indian civilization begins in about 1500 BC by an invasion of nomadic foreigners called the Aryans. According to this theory—now famous as the Aryan invasion theory—Indian civilization, beginning with the Vedic Age has always been a foreign imposition. This has been the central doctrine (and dogma) not only of former colonial rulers, but also of the dominant school of Indian historians in the half-century or so following independence.

It is not hard to see how this version came to be imposed during the colonial era: the British sought to make their own rule acceptable to Indians by claiming that India had always been ruled by foreigners, beginning with the Aryans themselves. Since Christian missionaries, many of whom were theologians rather than scientists, ran educational institutions, it was natural that a theological version of history around the doctrine of Aryan invasion should have been created. They modified Indian records to be in conformity with Biblical beliefs. The date of 1500 BC for the invasion by Aryans was fixed, based on the prevailing Biblical belief that world was created on 23 October 4004 BC! They were after all Christian priests, not scientists. This theological version had also the support of the ruling authorities.

Post colonial historians

Following Indian independence, Indian scholars had the opportunity to correct this century old imposition by going back to the original sources like the Vedas and the Puranas, supplemented by new discoveries in archaeology. Some like K.D. Sethna, Bhagwan Singh, Kailash Chandra Varma, Suraj Prakash Gupta, B.B. Lal, Udaya Veera Shastry and a few others did indeed do so. But their voices were drowned out in the din of influential historians who chose to stay with the colonial version, which was adopted to fit a new theology called Marxism. This happened because

Marxism and Marxist scholarship enjoyed official the patronage of left leaning politicians who ruled India. This gave rise to a school of leftist historians that through patronage and political influence came to dominate the writing and teaching of Indian history along Marxist lines. Independent minded historians who followed their own path became marginalized. They were like Vavilov and his geneticist colleagues pushed aside by Lysenko and his supporters.

For nearly fifty years following independence, this Marxist model has been the official version of ancient Indian history. Marx, being a product of nineteenth century Europe claimed that Indian civilization had never originated anything; this was simply his prejudice, for he knew nothing about India. In any event, this model holds Indian civilization—beginning with the Vedas—to be a foreign imposition. Since Marxism became the reigning ideology with influential Indian intellectuals, and also had official backing, it was never subjected to critical analysis. In the absence of debate, the Marxist version became the official version that is still found in history books. This is no different from what happened to genetics under Lysenko.

At this point it is worth noting that Indian literature knows nothing about this invasion: our Vedic ancestors—the Aryans—know of no homeland but India. Although the Vedas and the Puranas have been memorized and preserved for thousands of years, the same people have no memory of having come from any foreign land. Also, there is no archaeological evidence for such a massive invasion in ancient times. (This is discussed later in the book.) But we are asked to believe that the Aryans, generations of whom were able to memorize and orally preserve voluminous records like the Vedas and the Puranas for thousands of years, were incapable of remembering the name of their homeland. Their memory was so bad that they thought India itself was their original home. This is only the first of the contradictions.

As we shall see in this book, discoveries in archaeology and several other disciplines including natural history and genetics emphatically contradict the Aryan invasion idea. Members of the leftist school of historians—they no longer advertise their Marxist creed—are now engaged in a fierce battle with archaeologists and scientists to somehow preserve their crumbling theories and hold on to their influence in the face of the mounting body of evidence against them. But this is only to be expected, considering how much is at stake. This has now been joined by some American and European academics concerned about their continued survival.[1]

This fight against scientific evidence captures the essence of the theological approach: their doctrine is made to take precedence over facts and evidence exactly as in the time of Galileo. Some linguists also, especially in the West, with their linguistic theories too based on the Aryan invasion idea, are trying to hold on to the same doctrine. Thus it is not surprising that Marxist historians are now claiming that their theories are supported by linguistic evidence—never mind that the whole baggage of Indo-European linguistics was built assuming the Aryan invasion to be a fact. To now claim that linguistics supports the Aryan invasion is to be trapped in a circular argument.

Two approaches to history

To see the divide between the two approaches to history—the theological and the scientific—one can scarcely do better than compare the statements of a linguistic theologian and an empirical scientist. The late Murray Emeneau, a well-known linguist claimed:

> This [Aryan invasion] is our linguistic doctrine, which has been held now for more than a century and a half. There seems to be no reason to distrust the arguments for it, in spite of the traditional Hindu ignorance of any such invasion...

In making this claim Emeneau spoke not so much as a scientist as a theologian holding on to a doctrine. In fact, he admitted that he had no evidence for his doctrine; it has to be accepted on faith. On the other hand, when archaeologist Jim Shaffer says:

> Current archaeological data do not support the existence of an Indo-Aryan or European invasion into South Asia any time in the pre- or protohistoric periods...

Shaffer is expressing his view as an empirical scientist looking at the evidence before him. This shows the fundamental difference between science and theology.

---

[1]Two recent developments have made their case all but untenable. First, the admission in a BBC program that the idea was a British colonial concoction; second, genetic evidence showing next to Africa, India contains the oldest human populations. See Supplement I for a summary.

In addition, linguistics (or philology) is not a quantitative science. It cannot be used to determine dates of events that took place thousands of years ago. The unsoundness of using qualitative arguments from subjects like philology and theology for problems that demand scientific precision and quantitative methods has been recognized by all leading scientists and historians of science. The great British scientist Lord Kelvin wrote:

> ...when you can measure what you are speaking about, and express it in numbers, you know something about it; when you cannot measure it, when you cannot express it in numbers, your knowledge is of a meagre and unsatisfactory kind. (Merton, Sills and Stigler, 1984)

This is now famous as the 'Kelvin Dictum'. In this book we shall be following the path of the scientist, not the theologian. As far as possible, we shall base our conclusions on scientific methods when speaking of facts and dates. We shall be referring to the theologians only to point out their fallacies and highlight the risks in following their approach.

There are two major lessons to be learnt from a scientific study of ancient history and historiography. First, a proper understanding of ecology and natural history—not social or linguistic theories—holds the key to understanding ancient civilizations. Second, theology is the most deceptive of disciplines; it carries an appearance of sound logic but rests on no empirical foundation. Theology is useful not for discovering the truth, but for advancing a preconception built on a dogma; this often leads to concealment of truth and even falsification while creating an illusion of logical rigor. Ancient Greeks called such reasoning 'sophistry'. Hindus called it *mithyaa-vaada,* meaning false erudition.

What about Indology?

Readers of this book will be aware of the field called Indology that came into existence during the colonial period.[2] Much of what Indian students learn today about their ancient history derives from it. Most of us were brought up to believe that Western scholars beginning with Sir William Jones and his discovery of Sanskrit, culminating in the work of the Anglo-German F. Max Müller. Though a forgotten figure in Europe, educated Indians still revere him as a paragon of virtue and objective scholarship.

For reasons that we need not go into here, Indians tend to be naïve in

[2]Indology is a highly developed brand of what the late Edward Said called Orientalism.

judging Western scholars and their motives, attributing to them qualities that ignore common human traits like ambition, prejudice and the like that are part of everyone's makeup. This is particularly the case with Max Müller who is projected as a larger than life figure as a selfless scholar. Although his work is not without value he was human like anyone else. This is something we cannot ignore in evaluating the work of anyone, especially in a field like history, in which human feelings intrude upon the work to a much greater degree than they do in the exact sciences.

To understand how the currently popular notions about ancient India and its 'Aryan' creators were discovered, we need to go back to the Calcutta Judge (of the East India Company) Sir William Jones in the last decades of the eighteenth century. One of Jones's discoveries was that Indian languages—Sanskrit in particular—and European languages are related. To account for this, European scholars, the most famous of whom was F. Max Müller, proposed an invasion of 'Aryans' from the Eurasian steppes.

There were other currents—like colonial politics and Christian missionary interests—that need not detain us here. He assigned a date of 1500 BC for the invasion and 1200 BC for the composition of the *Rigveda*. The reason for the date was his firm belief in the Biblical chronology that assigned 23 October 4004 BC for the Creation and c. 2448 BC for Noah's Flood, though he sought to give other—equally fanciful—explanations. Though their facility with the Vedas and the Sanskrit language was likened by the great Dayananda Saraswati to a "toddler learning to walk," European scholars contrived to find and interpret a few passages in the Vedas as the record of the invasion of fair skinned Aryans and their victory over the dark skinned natives. In other words, the Aryan invaders were colonizers like themselves. As often the case, such theories tell us more about the people who created them than about history.

What the subject called European Indology brought to the study of ancient India was not so much science and scientific method as theology and rhetorical skills. It is the latter skills, which their modern Indian followers, Marxists especially, have mistaken for the scientific approach. Laws of nature pay no heed to rhetoric. It is of little value in any scientific study, for *nature is not fooled by clever rhetoric*. Anyone who cares about the search for truth must beware dogma and political operators masquerading as scholars.

To place Indology in proper perspective, one can say that it was driven by two motives: first, it gave the disunited and dispirited German people a theme for national unity; next it became a convenient platform for the British to build scientific sounding theories to justify their rule in India under the cover of the 'White Man's Burden.' This allowed them to pose as the protectors of their long lost Indian Aryan brothers who needed to be uplifted from their degraded state. (See Supplement I.)

These theories were racial in essence, but following Hitler and the Nazi atrocities, Western academics have become sensitive to charges of racism. They now advance the same theories, ideas and even the same conclusions under names like anthropology, Indo-European Studies and the like. Most recently, the names of genetics and genome research have been dragged into the scene to support these discredited nineteenth century ideas. This though amounts to little more than namedropping. Genetics, when properly applied, shows their theories to be false.

Once we recognize these facts and approach history with an open mind, the picture of ancient India that we get from science is very different from the one that political and missionary interests have created. It is also far more dramatic.

2.

Sarasvati: River lost and found

The Vedic Harappans

Our story begins with the fabled river Sarasvati, until recently thought to be a mythical river. Its importance arises from the fact that its discovery, or rather the discovery that the Sarasvati is no myth but a river that actually flowed thousands of years ago has completely changed our ideas about what the Vedic civilization was really like, and also when actually it flourished. For one thing it showed that the great river described in the Vedic literature, but no longer visible, was a victim of the changing ecology of North India more than four thousand years ago. At a technical level, the discovery showed that the famous Indus Valley Civilization (or the Harappan Civilization) owed more to the now dry Sarasvati than to the Indus. More of this later, but first we need to know something about the Indus Valley or the Harappan Civilization.

Most history books in India begin with an account of the famous cities of Harappa and Mohenjo Daro, now in Pakistan, and the Indus Valley (or the Harappan) Civilization to which they belonged. We now have many more sites on both sides of the border like Lothal, Dholavira and others. What is remarkable is that most of these went into decline and the whole civilization, spread over more than a million square kilometers, collapsed over a relatively short period. The reason given in most history books is the invasion of nomadic people who called themselves Aryas. This is the famous Aryan Invasion Theory, still found in one form or another in most history books and encyclopedias. The date given for the invasion is about 1500 BC.

This is supposed to be based on the literary record of the Aryans, the most important of which is the *Rigveda*. An immediate consequence of this theory is that both the Vedic people—as the Aryans should really be called—and their language (Vedic Sanskrit) were said to be of foreign origin. Since Harappan cities were flourishing more than a thousand years before the supposed arrival of the Aryans in India, it means that the Harappans, i.e., the inhabitants of the Harappan Civilization, must have been non-Vedic. This is an inescapable conclusion of the Aryan invasion theory.[1]

The discovery of the Sarasvati River dealt it a severe blow. It showed that the Sarasvati River, which supported the Harappan Civilization, was none other than the great river described in the *Rigveda.* This means that the Harappans were Vedic. Put another way, what it means is that the cities and other archaeological remains of the Harappan civilization represent the material side of the culture and civilization described in the Vedas.

That is to say, *the people who created the Vedic literature created also the Harappan cities.*

This means that the language of the Harappans and of the Vedic people were also the same. It is necessary therefore to take a closer look at the Harappans as well as the Sarasvati River.

Decline and fall of the Harappans

The discovery of Harappa and Mohenjo Daro in the early twenties of this century marks a watershed in the study of ancient history. These ancient sites revealed the existence of a vast civilization spread over more than a million square kilometers, exceeding in size and sophistication Egypt and Mesopotamia combined. This is now famous as the Harappan Civilization or the Indus Valley Civilization. Its discovery brought into question the whole foundation of ancient Indian history built around the Aryan invasion. Historians at first tried to make the ending of the Harappan Civilization coincide with the date of the Aryan invasion in 1500 BC and used it as support for the theory. This is now recognized to be several centuries too late. After applying the necessary corrections and calibrations it is impossible to place the ending of the mature Harappan Civilization any later than 1800 BC, while the most recent data indicate that even this may be too late by a century or more.

---

[1]This accounts for the fierce resistance to any suggestion or even evidence indicating that Harappan archaeology shows Vedic influence, especially in Western academia. The most vocal is probably the German-born Harvard linguist Michael Witzel who is an advocate of Aryan theories, which used to be popular in nineteenth century Germany and reached their culmination with the Nazis. This has now been demolished by genetics and the British admission that the whole thing was a colonial concoction. See Supplement I: The current state of Aryan theories.

On the latest evidence, 3000–2000 BC may be taken as a convenient estimate for the mature Harappan Civilization. (This is a rough approximation, with most scholars opting for 3100–1900 BC. Others claim that the mature phase of the Harappans began only in 2800 or 2700 BC. This is a matter of detail, depending on what one chooses to call 'mature', 'early', and so forth. Such hair splitting does not change the fact that archaeology records an advanced civilization in the same geographical region as the one described by the Vedic literature.)

These dates should be seen as approximate but have scientific support. Previous claims on the other hand were based on Biblical beliefs, linguistic theories and political expediency. The important point is that archaeologists have failed to find any records of destruction that could point to any invasion as the cause. The Vedic literature also knows no such invasion. The notion of any invasion is now contradicted by science. As American archaeologist Jim Shaffer noted:

> [C]urrent archaeological data do not support the existence of an Indo-Aryan or European invasion into South Asia anytime in the pre- or proto-historic periods. Instead, it is possible to document archaeologically a series of cultural changes reflecting indigenous cultural developments from prehistoric to historic periods. (Shaffer 1984: p 88)

In addition to this negative evidence, we also have much positive evidence that emphatically shows the Harappan Civilization to have been part of the Vedic Aryan fold. And this evidence includes remains attesting to the presence of horses. Advocates of the foreign origin of the Vedic Civilization have made much of the fact that horse remains have been found in the Eurasian steppes to claim that as the home of the Aryans. To press this claim they have coined the slogan: "No horse at Harappa."

This is demonstrably false. Horse remains—both domestic and the wild variety—have been found at places like Koldihwa and Mahagara in the interior of India dating to before 6500 BC! These are neolithic sites. The issue of the horse has been blown out of proportion by scholars with a vested interest in preserving the invasion theory and the non-indigenous basis of the Vedas and the Vedic civilization.[2] (We shall be devoting some

---

[2]One of the leaders of this denial is again Michael Witzel, who has gone on to claim that any evidence that shows the presence of the horse in Harappan remains is a later introduction. This means that the horse remains found and described by Sir John Marshall in the 1920s were introduced later! It has already been noted that Witzel and his school, if it can be called that, have been fully discredited, vide Supplement I.

attention to it in due course.) As S.R. Rao, one of the world's foremost archaeologists has pointed out:

> The negative evidence in the form of absence of the horse and rice in the Indus Civilization which was taken as evidence of its Dravidian origin no is longer tenable in view of the occurrence of horse bones and rice at Lothal, Kalibangan, Surkotada and Ropar in India and Mohenjo-Daro in Pakistan. On the other hand, there is enough positive evidence in support of the religious rites of the Harappans being similar to those of the Vedic Aryans. Their religious motifs, deities and sacrificial altars bespeak of Aryan faith. (*In* Talageri 1993: p vii)

Nor is this the whole story. They have been known in India from untold antiquity—a fact based on hard evidence. As a result, the dogma of "No horse at Harappa" has been demolished by science. As we shall see in a later chapter, far from supporting the Aryan invasion (or migration), *the horse evidence furnishes one of its strongest refutations*. In any event, it is minor sideshow and not central to our investigation.

When we examine the picture as a whole, what we see is that in the past few decades we have an accumulating body of data from several sources pointing to ecological degradation of large parts of North India and West Asia. This helps account for the rapid disintegration of both the Harappan and the nearby Akkadian empire of Mesopotamia. As a result of important explorations carried out by H. Weiss of Yale University, Mary-Ann Courty of CNRS France, along with those of several Indian and Western archaeologists including S.R. Rao and Jim Shaffer, it is safe to say that the end of the Harappan Civilization was brought about by forces of nature. It is now possible to ascribe it to global climate change—a gradual loss of water due to the drying up of the sources. This long desiccation process culminated in a severe drought that struck in the 2200–1900 BC interval. This great natural calamity affected ancient civilizations across an immense belt from the Aegean in southern Europe to India, going as far as China.

This now helps put an end to all speculation relating to the Aryan invasion as the cause of the collapse of the Harappan Civilization. It is beginning to be recognized that what ended the Vedic Age was not any invasion but the drying up of the Sarasvati—an event that was first placed at 1900 BC, but which may now have to be pushed back beyond 2000 BC based on the latest data. In any event we may conveniently take 2000 BC for the date of *complete* drying up of the Sarasvati River.

The 'Great Drought' of 2200–1900 BC: global calamity

The drying up of the Sarasvati River was part of a global phenomenon that severly impacted ancient civilizations in a vast belt from the Aegean (southern Europe) to India, reaching as far as China. This is recognized to have taken place in the 2200–1900 BC period. It was this calamity and not any invasion that caused the collapse of the Harappan Civilization. It is necessary to keep this ecological picture in mind when we look at ancient civilizations, including the Vedic and the Harappan.

It is widely recognized that the Sarasvati was the Vedic river *par excellence.* This at one stroke places the Vedic Civilization also before 2000 BC. Since the mature or the 'high' Harappan Civilization is also known to have ended around the same time (and *not* 1500 BC as often stated in history books), it makes the Harappan and the Vedic Civilizations overlap at least towards the end of both; the two ended at the same time. And the cause was also the same—the Great Drought of 2200–1900 BC. But the story does not end here for the situation is far more dramatic as we now learn by piecing together data from several significant archaeological and satellite studies.

The first of these is the recently concluded joint French-American study in northern Mesopotamia just noted (Weiss, Courty et. al. 1993). They have found that the Akkadian empire of Mesopotamia, which had extensive trade contacts with the Harappans was brought to an abrupt end as the result of a severe drought that began in about 2200 BC and persisted for nearly 300 years. They attribute this to a global climatic change of increasing aridity that began nearly a thousand years earlier climaxing in what was the Great Drought of c. 2200–1900 BC.[3]

This also helps account for the near simultaneous collapse of the far-flung Harappan Civilization. Floods and invasion do not cause the simultaneous abandonment of settlements stretching across more than a thousand kilometers, and yet this is exactly what we find at sites from Harappa to Lothal to Dholavira; they were all given up more or less simultaneously. S.R. Rao dates the abandonment of the mature Harappan cities to c. 1900 BC, which is probably an underestimate, but lies well within the calibration limits of dating techniques used by archaeologists.

---

[3]I am grateful to Dr. K.D. Prithipaul of the University of Alberta for bringing this to my attention.

There can be no doubt at all that the population was stressed. Weiss, Courty, et al. (1993: pp 995-1004) note this as being part of a collapse recorded across an immense belt that included the Aegean, Palestine, Egypt, India and of course Mesopotamia. We can once again take 2000 BC as a convenient if rough marker. Keeping this in background, we may next look at what the Sarasvati was like in ancient times and what it meant to the Vedic people.

Sarasvati, the best mother

Of the many important discoveries made since 1975 or so, the discovery of the Sarasvati River, first indicated by satellite photos, and later confirmed on the ground in a great expedition led by the late V.S. Wakankar, is probably the most important. I already noted that the discovery of the Sarasvati is a major blow to the Aryan invasion theory. It is time now to take another look at this extraordinarily important development. Let us first try to locate it based on current knowledge and ancient literature. It should be kept in mind, however, that we keep on getting new data, and any explanation will have to be updated every few years.

V.S. Wakankar

The *Rigveda* gives great importance to the Sarasvati, even more than what we now give the Ganga. While the Ganga receives only one mention, the Sarasvati is mentioned at least sixty times. In one Rigvedic verse

(VII.4.8)[4], Vasishta describes the Sarasvati as "purest among the rivers, flowing from the mountains to the sea." Also, she captured the Drishadvati as a tributary, sanctifying the land between the two rivers, making it the "holiest place on earth." This region later came to be known as Kurukshetra or the seat of the Kurus. Earliest it seems to have been known as Ilavarta. Ila is another name for the Sarasvati, and Ilavarta means surrounded by Ila or the Sarasvati.

The Sarasvati was not only the holiest river, but also the greatest. According to Bharadwaja of the sixth book (VI.61.2), the Sarasvati in flowing through the mountains "crushed boulders like stems of lotus plants." From all this we learn that the Sarasvati was the greatest river, the most holy and also sustained large populations. This idea finds expression in the following verse by Gritsamada (VI.41.16):

ambītame, nadītame, devītame sarasvati.

That is, the Sarasvati was "the best of mothers, the best river, the best goddess." In the light of all this, we could term the Vedic civilization the Sarasvati civilization. In fact, this is how the poets of the *Rigveda* describe their land and the culture—as the gift of the Sarasvati. Some modern scholars, however, claim that the Sarasvati is really the river Haraqiti in Afghanistan. According to this view, the memory of this river, actually a quite insignificant stream, was brought to India by the invading Aryans, who celebrated it as Sarasvati. This has two major problems. The Haraqiti in landlocked Afghanistan does not flow "from the mountains to the sea," as described in the *Rigveda.* More serious is the location: the famous *Nadi Sukta* of the *Rigveda* (X.75.5) places the Sarasvati between the Yamuna and the Shutudri (Sutlej). Enumerating the rivers from east to west, it says:

imam me gange yamune sarasvatī shutudrī stomam parushnyā;
asiknyā marudvridhe vitastyā arjikiye shrinuhyā sushomayā.

Since the *Nadi Sukta* mentions all the rivers from the Ganga to the Indus and beyond, locating the Sarasvati in Afghanistan would require us to shift the Ganga, Yamuna and other Indian rivers also to Afghanistan. More importantly, the passage helps us locate the Sarasvati—between the Yamuna and the Sutlej.

---

[4]In referring to passages in the *Rigveda,* the first term (in Roman numerals) indicates the book or the *mandala,* the second the hymn or the *sukta,* and the third the verse of the mantra. For example, X.75.5 refers to mantra 5 in *sukta* 75 from the tenth book or *mandala* X of the *Rigveda.*

However, there is now no river answering to this description. This has led scholars to dismiss it as the imagination of poets. This is not easy, considering that not only the *Rigveda* but also later literature like the Brahmanas and even the *Mahabharata* describe it and the surrounding landscape in detail. From the later literature we also learn that the Sarasvati was no longer the mighty river described in the *Rigveda,* and had actually split into two parts.

All of this can be learned from deşcriptions found in the Vedic and the epic and Puranic literature. Scientific investigations were not long in coming, even in the nineteenth century. As far back as 1886, R.J. Oldham of the Geological Survey of India concluded that a great river with its course lying between the Yamuna and the Sutlej did exist in ancient times as described in the *Rigveda.* He located its upper course along the seasonal stream Ghaggar-Sarasvati in Haryana. He also noted that there were significant differences between the Sarasvati of the *Rigveda* and the Sarasvati described in the later literature. Oldham based his conclusions on the similarity of fossil remains along the course of the dry riverbed.

Oldham's work was ignored by most historians who remained attached to the idea that the Vedic Aryans came to India in 1500 BC and composed the *Rigveda* in 1200 BC. And the Sarasvati was only their favourite deity worshipped in the form of the river. This of course is part of the century-old now discredited Aryan invasion theory. Then in the twentieth century, when archaeologists discovered the Harappan Civilization, there were more problems with the Aryan invasion idea.

Excavations found a large number of Harappan settlements not on the Indus, but at locations from 40 to 120 kilometres to the east of it. Hundreds of sites have been found in Cholistan in the Bahawalpur district of Pakistan. Today, there is no major water source in the region, but there must have been some when these sites were flourishing.. The same situation is encountered in parts of Rajashtan and Kutch, of ancient settlements in areas where there is little water today. All this suggests that a major river must have been flowing through the region in ancient times. The most logical explanation that the source that fed this civilization was the Sarasvati described in the ancient literature.

All this may be seen only as circumstantial evidence arguing for the existence of the Sarasvati. Beginning in 1978, direct evidence also became available in the form of satellite images acquired by earth sensing satellites launched by NASA (National Aeronautics and Space

Administration) and ISRO (Indian Space Research Organization). These images showed traces of ancient river courses (called palaeo-channels) that lay along the course of the Sarasvati River described in the ancient literature. They showed a channel ranging in width from 6 to 8 kilometres, exceeding 14 kilometres in places. This raises two basic questions. First, when did this river dry up and why? Second, since the bulk of the so-called Harappan (or Indus) settlements are found along the course of the Sarasvati River rather than the Indus, would it not be more appropriate to call it the Sarasvati civilization? (It is now called the Indus-Sarasvati civilization.)

In any event, we already saw that the Vedic civilization was nourished by the Sarasvati. This is what the *Rigveda* tells us. The same we now know was true of the Harappan (or the Indus) Civilization, which flourished in the 3100–1900 BC period. What then was the nature of the relationship between these two civilizations—both of which were nurtured by the Sarasvati? This may be seen as the central question of ancient Indian history. Efforts to answer this has led to far-reaching advances in our understanding of ancient India, including its geography.

The next question is what was the Sarasvati like in Rigvedic times? More broadly, since rivers have changed courses, what was Rigvedic geography like? In other words, what was the geography of North India as described in the *Rigveda,* especially the rivers?

Rigveda decribes pre-Harappan geography

We should note once and for all that these findings put an end to all speculation concerning the 'Aryan invasion' as the cause of the end of the Harappan Civilization. The mature Harappan Civilization came towards the end of the Vedic Age and was part of it. The two ended together and for the same reason—an ecological calamity of epic proportions. This is the picture we get when we look at some recent scientific findings (see page 17).

This now helps also solve one of the great puzzles stemming from some other studies, notably the Indo-French satellite cum field study reported by Paul-Henri Francfort of CNRS, France (Francfort 1992). Note that the Sarasvati is supposed to have dried up around 2000 BC. But what follows from the Indo-French field study is something quite different: *no perennial river had flown in the area for over a thousand years.* The Sarasvati as a great river is well attested by satellite pictures taken by the

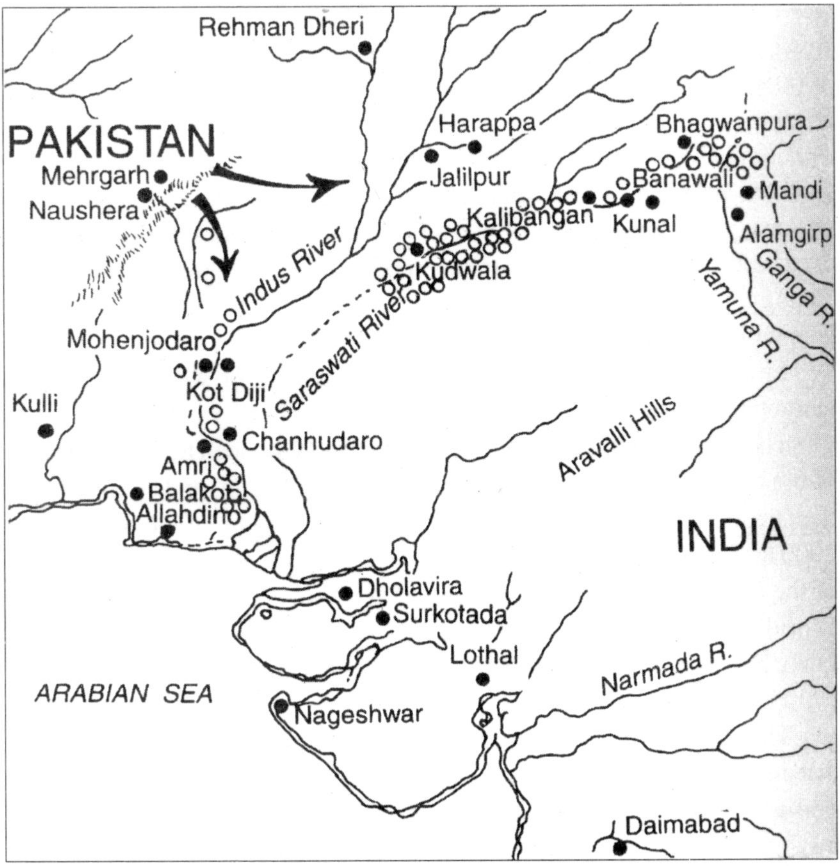

NASA satellite Landsat; it had a constant width varying from six to eight kilometers, extending in places to fourteen kilometers. This corresponds to the river described in the *Rigveda.* (In the 1980s, I worked extensively with Landsat images at NASA.)

Francfort, however, pointed to the presence of Proto Harappan sites (or Early Harappan, c. 3000 BC and earlier) found on the riverbed itself. This shows that the river must have been dry for some centuries before these sites could be established. The same is true of its northern tributary the Drishadvati (Chautang), which is also mentioned in the *Rigveda.* This can only mean that the Sarasvati and the Drishadvati must both have been dry for several centuries before 3000 BC, at least in areas where those early settlements have been found on the riverbeds. Both these rivers are mentioned in the *Rigveda.*

Thus the geography described by the *Rigveda* in which the Sarasvati flowed from 'the mountain to the sea' is seen to have been long before 3000 BC. The fact that the Sarasvati split into fragments due to the encroachment of the desert is noted in such post Vedic works as the *Panchavimsa Brahmana,* the *Mahabharata* as well as in the *Puranas* as we shall see later. This means that the *Rigveda* describes the geography of the regions, when the Sarasvati flowed from "the mountains to the sea," as it used to be during the pre-Harappan period. This is what the one known example of pre-Harappan writing also suggests. (This is described in the chapter on the Indus script.)

In other words, the *Rigveda* is pre-Harappan, or what is the same, Harappan archaeology is post Rigvedic.

The drying up of the Sarasvati may therefore be seen to have been part of the global climatic change that began before 3000 BC and culminated in the Great Drought in 2200 BC. The *complete* drying up of the Sarasvati in 2000 BC (or 1900 BC) was not an isolated event in space or in time, but part of the overall ecological degradation that afflicted a large part of the Old World. This places the High Sarasvati Civilization—as the Vedic may fairly be described—firmly before even the beginning of the Harappan of c. 3000–2000 BC.

This is only the beginning, for the Sarasvati itself, before it completely dried up shortly after 2000 BC, went through two phases: first, the phase during which the Rigvedic age flourished, when the northern course was mighty and nourished the Sarasvati-Drishadvati doab, or the sacred land later known as Kurukshetra. The next phase was the post-Rigvedic, Harappan period, when the ancient Sarasvati disappeared at a place called Vinashana near the present day Kalibangan in Rajasthan, but a western course flowed through parts of Rajasthan, Sindh all the way to the Rann of Kutch. This is the course along which the bulk of the settlements of the Harappan period have been found. We may call this the Harappan Sarasvati to distinguish from the Vedic Sarasvati.

Sarasvati River and Civilization[5]

Once satellite data established the existence of the Sarasvati, several archaeologists undertook the task of locating its course on the ground by

[5]A valuable source for this information is *Vedic Sarasvati: Evolutionary history of a lost river of Northwestern India* edited by B.P. Radhakrishna and S.S. Mehr, published by the Geological Society of India.

correlating satellite data with ground observations. A leading figure among these was the late V.S. Wakankar already known for his discovery of pre-historic cave paintings at Bhimbhetka in Madhya Pradesh. He led a multidisciplinary team of experts on a 4000-kilometre exploration from the Himalayas to the Rann of Kutch. This and succeeding investigations have shed a good deal of new light on the Sarasvati and the civilizations it gave rise to.

To begin with, the great Sarasvati River described in the *Rigveda* as flowing from the "mountains to the sea" is very ancient, several centuries before 3000 BC or well over 5000 years old, as we have already seen. What is interesting is that the Yamuna (a tributary of the Ganga), and the Sutlej (a tributary of the Indus) then flowed into the Sarasvati. This made the river mighty. Sometime before 3000 BC, probably due to tectonic shifts that followed earthquakes, the Yamuna changed its course and began to flow into the Ganga. This reduced the flow into the Sarasvati, leading to a weakening of its upper course that soon disappeared into the desert at a place called Vinashana. Archaeologists have identified the place as Kalibangan in Rajashtan where Harappan and pre-Harappan settlements have been found, along with signs of at least one earthquake. This corresponds to the description found in the post *Rigveda* literature like the *Jaiminiya Brahmana* and also the *Mahabharata.*

While the upper Sarasvati weakened and disappeared into the desert, the lower Sarasvati continued to flow through what is now the Thar Desert, fed by the Sutlej and other rivers. This is what sustained the Harappan settlements in Rajasthan, Sindh and Cholistan down to the Rann of Kutch. But this Sarasvati too dried up in stages in the 2200–1900 BC period, ending with it the Harappan civilization. The reason for this was ecological degradation and not any invasion—Aryan or otherwise. First, as had happened with the Yamuna earlier, the Sarasvati lost the Sutlej, when it changed its course and became a tributary of the Indus. This was compounded by a massive worldwide drought in the 2200–1900 BC period that struck across a wide belt from southern Europe to China. It ended the civilizations of Dynastic Egypt and Sumer-Akkad in Mesopotamia along with the Harappan. (The Harappan civilization ended around 1900 BC, not 1500 BC as stated in some history books.)

We may summarize the situation as follows: the Sarasvati described in the *Rigveda* flowed through the Ghaggar channel—what is now a seasonal stream in Haryana. It had two major tributaries—the Sutlej and the

Yamuna. The Yamuna, or a major effluent of it, flowed into the Sarasvati via the Chautang channel. Chautang too is a seasonal stream today. This made the Sarasvati mighty. Some centuries before 3000 BC, if not a good deal earlier, the Yamuna shifted and began to flow into the Ganga. Then, a few centuries later, the Sutlej (called Shutudri in the *Rigveda*) also shifted course and began to flow as an independent river by joining the Beas. This deprived the Sarasvati of its two major sources and it became an insignificant river, though the memory of its glory days remained. The *Rigveda* of course describes the Sarasvati in its full glory.

The situation then was that the Sutlej-Beas, flowing as an independent river all the way to the Rann of Kutch, supported the Harappan Civilization in the period from about 3100 BC to 1900 BC. Then a twin disaster struck: the Sutlej shifted course again, westward, becoming a tributary of the Indus, and the Great Drought of 2200–1900 BC struck the region, bringing the Harappan civilization to an end. This is a simplified, possibly oversimplified, account of a long and tortuous ecological process.

This was a devastating blow to the ecology of the region. This resulted in the migration of its inhabitants south to Gujarat and also west into West Asia. There are records of Kassite rulers, apparently of Indian origin, establishing an empire in Babylon that lasted more than 500 years. A major development following the complete drying up of the Sarasvati was the loosening of the common Vedic bond over North India giving rise to regional cultures and small political units known as Janapadas. This is the picture we get from Buddhist and Jain literature. Regional languages, often called Prakrits came into prominence while Sanskrit receded into the background. It is no accident that we find Buddhist and Jain works written mostly in Prakrits like Pali and Ardhamagadhi—rarely in Sanskrit.

Ancient chronology: the Harappa-Sutra connection

The basic point to note is that culturally the Vedic and Harappan civilizations were one and the same, both nourished by the Sarasvati, but distinguished ecologically by the shifting fortunes of the Sarasvati River. This gave rise to two related but ecologically distinct hydrological zones. The Rigvedic Sarasvati represents a different (earlier) phase of the river from the one that made the Harappan civilization possible. Culturally the sites belonging to the Harappan Civilization are part of the Vedic Aryan civilization, though of course of a later phase. S.R. Rao in India, A.H. Dani in Pakistan and several others have found evidence of Vedic practices including sacrifices and fire worship. A careful correlation of these archaeological finds like Vedic altars with the technical literature has shown that the *Sulbasutras*—which are mathematical manuals found in the Vedic literature—must have been used in their design and construction. Thus both archaeology and the Vedic literature must have been part of the same civilization. (This is discussed in more detail in the section on the Vedic Harappans in a later chapter.)

These mathematical texts are part of the so-called Sutra period of the Vedic Age. The four Vedas constitute the basic Vedic literature. These were followed the Brahmanas and the Sutras. The Sutra period is therefore the closing part of the Vedic Age. The famous *Sulbasutras* (or the Sulbas) are part of the Sutra literature and therefore came at the end of the Vedic Age. Since we now have connections between the Sulbas and Harappan archaeology, this suggests that the Harappan Civilization must also have belonged to the closing period of the Vedic Age.

This conclusion is now supported by other research. On the basis of a comparison of archaeology with the literary records of India and Mesopotamia, K.D. Sethna and others have independently shown that the Harappan Civilization of c. 3000 to 2000 BC corresponds also to the Sutra period of the Vedic literature. The Harappans carried on brisk trade with the Sumerians who had their own empire in the valleys of the rivers Tigris and Euphrates in West Asia. This region is often called Mesopotamia. Sethna's work is based on a comparison of Indian and Sumerian records, and may briefly be summarized as follows.[6]

Sethna noted that the evidence of cotton in Sumeria and at Harappan sites, combined with references to cotton for the first time in the Sutra literature imply that both the Harappan and the Sumerian-Akkadian civilizations belong to the Sutra period. He was able to determine this by noting the fact that the Sanskrit word *karpasa* for cotton becomes *kapazum* in Sumerian (Akkadian). Further, Sumerian records are clear that cotton—*kapazum*—was a commodity imported from India. Sethna also noted that the country from which *kapazum*-cotton was imported was known as *Meluhha*—pronounced 'melukha'. This is a corruption of the Prakrit word 'Malekha' which referred to the western parts of India. The Prakrit word Malekha itself is a corruption of Sanskrit 'Mleccha'—the term applied to the westerners in the Sutra and the Brahmana literature.

---

[6]See *KARPASA* by Sethna for more on the trade connections. For the role of the *Sulbasutras,* see *Vedic Aryans and the Origins of Civilization* by Rajaram and Frawley.

My own work based on the relationship between the *Sulbasutras* and the mathematics of Old-Babylonia (c. 1900–1750 BC) and the Egyptian Middle Kingdom (c. 2050–1800 BC) leads to the same conclusion. (I discuss this later in the book.) It is to be noted that our two derivations are completely independent: one uses mathematics, the other literary records. (And this is confirmed by the recent decipherment of the Indus script. We find mathematical expressions from the *Sulbasutras* on a few Indus seals.)

All this now gives us a fundamental chronological equation: the Sutra period, the mature Harappan Civilization and the Sumerian empire overlapped c. 3000–2000 BC. This also shatters the Max Müller chronology of 600–200 BC for the Sutra period, more of which later. But his date was based on 1200 BC for the *Rigveda,* which we now know to be late by at least 2000 years. So an error of the same magnitude with the date of the Sutra literature is only to be expected.

This means that the Sutra literature, in particular the mathematics of the *Sulbasutras,* must have been the basis for the great urban civilization of the Harappans. Without this scientific infrastructure the great urban civilization of the Harappans would have been impossible, just as the information age that characterizes our civilization would have been impossible without modern mathematics. This further means that the Harappan Civilization, just like the Sutra period, came at the end of the Vedic Age. Its end was brought about by global climatic change that culminated in a 300-year drought.

This allows us to arrive at a few preliminary chronological markers for the Vedic and Harappan societies that may be delineated on the basis of what we know about the Sarasvati. The important point to note is that the scientific analysis presented here shows that the *Rigveda* describes the society before the rise of the Harappan Civilization. This is the exact reverse of the chronological relationship between the Vedic and Harappan societies given in history books currently in use.

Rigvedic society: pastoral, urban or maritime?

This helps also clear up some of the confusion surrounding the Harappan society as revealed by archaeology and the one described in the *Rigveda.* Advocates of the foreign origin of the Vedic Aryans have tried to show that the *Rigveda* describes a society that is more pastoral and not one so highly urbanized. On the other hand, those who hold to an indigenous origin for the Vedic Civilization point to the presence of sacrificial altars and other signs pointing to Vedic Aryanism, as well as complete absence of evidence for any invasion in ancient times. (We can forget claims of "no horse at Harappan sites": it is patently false, as we shall see later in the book.)

To get to the main point of the dispute: both sides in the urban-pastoral debate are partially correct, and both have seen only parts of the picture. The urbanized society revealed by Harappan archaeology corresponds to the society described in the Sutra and the *Mahabharata* periods. The early Sutra authors know of the Mahabharata War. The *Rigveda* describes a society that is at least five hundred years earlier, a society less urbanized than the one revealed by Harappan archaeology. The early Vedic Age—of the four Vedas and the early Brahmanas—was more spiritual and less materialistic. The materialistic civilization described in the Sutras and the *Mahabharata* corresponds well with what we see in Harappan archaeology. The *Ramayana* on the other hand describes a society that is more ancient, not far removed from the *Rigveda.* The society described in the *Ramayana* is much less urbanized with many more forest dwellings. Cities did exist, but the society was less urbanized than the Harappan. The *Rigveda* also describes cities.

One Indian historian, R.S. Sharma, has repeatedly stressed that there appears to be a mismatch between the highly urbanized Harappan Civilization, and what he sees as the largely pastoral society described in the *Rigveda.* This is easily explained by the fact that the Harappan society corresponds to not the *Rigveda* but the later Vedic period, especially of the Sutras and the Upanishads. Sharma, an upholder of the Aryan invasion, is not being consistent when he places the supposedly pastoral Rigvedic society after the highly urbanized Harappan. It is easy to understand the urbanization of a pastoral society, but not so easy to see a highly urbanized society becoming pastoral. This should help clear up the confusion about the relationship between the Rigvedic and the Sutra periods. In any event, it is wrong to say that the Rigvedic society did not know cities.

However all this misses the real point: *the society described in the Rigveda had a significant maritime component.* The debate focusing on the pastoral-urban argument has completely missed the main message, which is: *the dominant imagery and symbolism of the Rigveda is not pastoral but oceanic.* This has been conclusively shown by David Frawley and now stands confirmed by archaeology. (See Foreword.)

This is not the place to go into details about the more enlightened reading of the *Rigveda* that is offered by David Frawley, which shows the pervasiveness of the ocean symbolism. The idea of Aryans as a nomadic-pastoral people is a nineteenth century misconception which now persists in the form of the urban-pastoral debate about the Harappans and the Rigvedic people. Once we drop this preconception and study the *Rigveda* with an open mind, the strong oceanic symbolism can hardly be missed.

At this point the reader may find it useful to go back to David Frawley's Foreword to the present book. Not only does it tell us that the Vedic people were a maritime people but also why; the Western tribes of the Aryans known as the Yadus were a largely maritime people who lived in the enormous riverine delta that stretched all along the seacoast from the mouth of the Narmada to that of the Indus. This includes both the Rann of Kutch and the Gulf of Khambhat in the present day Gujarat. Very ancient underwater settlements have recently been found in these parts. It lends further support to the maritme basis of the Vedic society.

I discuss all this in more detail later in Chapter 5. Those interested in learning more about the maritime nature of the Vedic people will find it interesting to read the discussion given in David Frawley's book *Gods, Sages and Kings*.

Digression on metals and ancient metallurgy

It is now possible to discern a clear pattern emerging from archaeology. As I noted earlier, some early Harappan sites are being found on the Sarasvati riverbed itself, which shows that the river in those areas must have been dry no later than 3000 BC. Numerous pre-Harappan sites on the other hand are located along the ancient course, which indicates that the Sarasvati must have been a still flourishing river at the time. Since the Vedas describe the Sarasvati as the greatest river and worship it as the holy mother, only these pre Harappan-sites, established before the river dried up, can belong to the civilization described in the Vedas. The same is true of the Drishadvati, another Vedic river.

The next question: can we correlate other scientific data with the literary accounts of the Vedic period? The discovery of pre-Harappan sites along the ancient Sarasvati shows that the Vedic Civilization—at least of the *Rigveda*—was predominantly pre Harappan. It also shows that we must give up the nineteenth century idea that the Vedic Aryans were nomads. Numerous settlements have been found along its course in Haryana and Rajasthan. A good number of these Sarasvati sites are pre-

Harappan, like the recently discovered one at Kunal in Haryana. This again confirms that the Vedic Civilization was also pre Harappan.

Most of these pre-Harappan sites are agricultural settlements and show no signs of having been populated by newcomers to the area. Kunal, a recently discovered Sarasvati site in Haryana has revealed silver ornaments. This shows that their metallurgy must have been quite advanced; unlike gold, silver never appears in pure form and has to be extracted by separating it from other metals like copper, zinc and lead. The date of Kunal is definitely earlier than 3000 BC. After suitable corrections and calibrations are applied, it will probably be assigned to before 3300 BC. The extraction of silver must therefore have been mastered well before that date.

While this is certainly a very early date, the presence of silver ornaments at Kunal—an early Sarasvati site—shows that it is still later than the society described in the *Rigveda.* This is because the *Rigveda* does not mention silver. The oldest Sanskrit word for silver is *rajatam hiranyam*—literally 'white gold'—and it is mentioned for the first time in the *Yajurveda.* When Rigvedic settlements are identified, in all probability metal artifacts occurring at those sites—like bronze and copper objects—will be found to contain silver as impurity indicating that separation of silver had not yet been mastered. Based on an analysis of both metallurgical and ecological data that is now available, I believe this date will prove to be no later than 3500 BC. Thus the presence of silver as impurity in copper and bronze artifacts may be taken as a convenient if approximate guide in identifying Rigvedic sites. (The term 'bronze' is not strictly correct; it is actually copper based natural alloy.)

At least one such artifact appears to be known. It is a very ancient casting found in 1958 by the American collector and history enthusiast Harry Hicks near Delhi now famous as 'Vasistha's Head'. It was thoroughly analyzed by him and the metallurgist Robert Anderson at laboratories in California and Switzerland. It has now been scientifically dated to 3800–3700 BC based on both radiocarbon (using particles of soot deposited during casting) and also by more modern metallic re-crystallization tests. Hicks and Anderson identify the Head as a possible likeness of Vasistha based on descriptions found in the *Rigveda.*

Their identification of it as a likeness of Vasistha is not easy to accept, but the date of the casting established on the basis of tests carried out at some of the leading laboratories of Europe and America appears to be reliable. Remarkably enough the casting does contain a high percentage of silver as impurity. Other data also suggest that it was extracted from sulfide ore, a typical source of silver. Both its date and its metallurgical composition—including silver impurity—make it a candidate for the period of the *Rigveda.* As a result, based on its scientifically determined date and its metallurgical profile, we may conclude that the so-called 'Vasistha's Head' was probably cast in the Rigvedic period. All of this now allows us to summarize the chronology of the Vedic Age as shown in the following chronological table. These dates, especially of the ending of the Rigvedic Age c. 3750 BC must be regarded as conservative.

Period	**Dates**	**Remarks**
Great Drought	2200-1900 BC	End of the ancient world
Sarasvati river end	2200-2000 BC?	Complete drying up of the Sarasvati river
Sutra-Harappa period	c. 3000-2000 BC	Age of the *Sulbasutras*
Sarasvati civilization	Before 3200 BC	Flourishing Sarasvati river
Introduction of silver, Kunal-discoveries	c. 3500 BC or earlier	The late Veda Brahmana period
Battle of Ten Kings: seventh and the third mandalas of the *Rigveda*	3750 BC	End of the Rigvedic Age Age of Vasistha and Viswamitra
Final end of the last Ice Age (Younger Dryas)	c. 8000 BC	Origins of the Vedic Age?

Chronological table from the Ice Age to the Great Drought

As a result of these developments it is safe to say that we are now in the midst of a fundamental change of paradigm in our study of ancient India. Qualitative methods based on linguistics and social and political theories—such as migrations and nomadism—are progressively giving way to more scientific methods based on the natural sciences and technology. At the most fundamental level, the crucial role of ecology in the rise and fall of civilizations is now getting better understood. A new methodology combining modern science and ancient records, exemplified by Wakankar's pioneering exploration of the Vedic Sarasvati River is promising to open new windows on the world's past.

To understand the Vedic Civilization properly it is necessary to look at the unfolding ecological picture of the Indian subcontinent beginning with the end of the last Ice Age. The last Ice Age ended some 10,000 years ago with rising temperatures releasing waters from the accumulated ice caps.[7] These ice caps had been building for more than a hundred thousand years. As the ice caps melted, it resulted in the discharge of enormous quantities of water into the Indian subcontinent in the form of numerous rivers and streams that have long since disappeared. For several thousand years North India was the beneficiary of this bounty of nature.

The legend of the periodic slaying of Vritra (the 'coverer') by the solar god Indra refers probably to this phenomenon—the periodic melting of ice caps with the arrival of spring. Photographs taken by the French satellite SPOT show that North India was then fed by an enormous number of natural streams. Many areas like Sind, Baluchistan and Rajasthan that are now arid were once fertile and supported agriculture. The Sarasvati was then the greatest of rivers exactly as described in the *Rigveda*. Over the next several thousand years the accumulated supply of water in the form of ice caps came to be depleted and deserts began to form. This culminated in the Great Drought of 2200–1900 BC that ended the Harappan Civilization. With its end the Vedic Age also ended.

Sarasvati lost and found

In summary, we may say that the loss of the Sarasvati was twofold: first the river disappeared until it was resurrected by science; and the civilization that it supported—the Harappan—was lost forever leaving only mute remains, who have begun to speak to us again thanks to more enlightened reading of its remains.

The rise and fall of the Vedic Civilization therefore is not to be attributed to any invasion—Aryan or otherwise—but to the long boom-and-bust ecological cycle that came at the end of the last Ice Age. The

[7]Recent discoveries show that the ending of the Ice Age was soon followed by a return of the freezing condition, which lasted several centuries. This is known as the Younger Dryas. The Vritra of the *Rigveda* refers probably to the recovery form this second brief Ice Age condition. This is somewhat technical, which I have discussed elsewhere. (See my article "History as an extension of natural history," cited in the Bibliography.

Harappan Civilization was the Vedic Twilight. Archaeology records a continuous and largely indigenous evolution going back to 7000 BC at sites like Mehrgarh. (This is now supplemented by even earlier underwater settlements off the coast of Gujarat in the west and Tamil Nadu in the east.) The *Rigveda* and the Vedic Civilization that gave birth to it were a unique human response to a unique natural age of water abundance in the immediate aftermath of the last Ice Age. This also goes to explain why maritime activity was so important.

In summary, the creator and the destroyer of the Vedic Age were one and the same—changing ecology: what nature giveth, nature taketh away.

3.

Colonial cobwebs: The Aryan problem

Cobwebs of colonialism

To get to the heart of the problem, to understand the origin and growth of Indian civilization, we need first to confront an issue that has dominated historical discourse in India: who were the Aryans? Were they members of a race as German nationalists in the nineteenth century and British rulers later told us? Or are they a linguistic and cultural group as Western scholars like Max Müller insisted? (Though, as we shall see later, he said both depending on the political circumstances.) More fundamentally, especially in today's context, were the Aryans and their civilization of Indian origin or were they brought by nomadic invaders some three or four thousand years ago?

These are questions that we need to address before we can expect to make any headway. For better or for worse, they are part of Indian historiography. As we shall soon see, these issues are part of the cobwebs of colonialism. They need first to be cleared before we can look at history in earnest.

Politics, superstition and science[1]

For more than a century, the history of ancient India has been written based on the Aryan invasion model. According to this theory, Indian history begins shortly after 1500 BC with the invasion of bands nomadic people from Central Asia called the Aryans. The theory holds the *Rigveda,* the most ancient and the most important of the Indian scriptures, to be the creation of these nomadic invaders, composed sometime after 1200 BC.

The first point to note is that the Aryan invasion theory is entirely a nineteenth century European creation. It finds no support in ancient Indian

[1]See *The Politics of History* by N.S. Rajaram for a more detailed discussion of these topics. It does not discuss some recent scientific findings, especially in genetics, that were not then available.

records, which recognize no homeland but India. Also, the theory was formulated at a time when there was no archaeology or scientific methods to assist nineteenth century European scholars who also for the most part lacked scientific education. Most of them believed in the Biblical theory of creation according to which the world with all its living beings was created at 9:00 AM on October 23, 4004 BC. For several centuries it was a serious offense for any Christian to question this dogma. Firm belief in this date led early Indologists to manipulate Indian history and chronology to fit everything within the framework of this Biblical superstition.

History books no longer mention this Biblical background—most authors are probably unaware of it—but unwittingly they still carry the legacy of this Christian Fundamentalist doctrine. It was later presented in linguistic terms, but the chronology of ancient India and the date of the *Rigveda* found in history books ultimately rest on these Biblical beliefs: Creation in 4004 BC and the Biblical Flood in 2448 BC. Nor is this the only contributor to the Aryan invasion theory as we shall soon discover. European politics and British colonial interests too played their role. These are inescapable facts, however much present day academics, especially in the West, may want everyone to forget it.

While the Aryan invasion theory is supposed to account for similarities between Sanskrit and European languages, lurking in the background were also some political ideas current in nineteenth century Europe, especially German nationalism.[2] The proponents of the Aryan invasion theory have been mainly linguists and anthropologists who continue to base their own formulations on nineteenth century theories. In doing so they have been guilty of ignoring other factors such as German nationalism and British colonial and Christian missionary interests that shaped it to a much greater degree than science or evidence. In fact, science played no role. On the other hand, it is contradicted by science, most recently by findings in population genetics.

These political considerations, and religious dogmas, far more than linguistic scholarship, were what went into its creation and official

[2]It is still held by some scholars, especially Europeans (like Michael Witzel) who remain wedded to nineteenth century ideas but claim to deny its racist doctrines. Also they no longer call it the Aryan invasion theory (AIT) but the Aryan migration theory (AMT). The latest entrant is the Aryan 'influx' theory so the AIT can be retained. In this verbal gymnastics the conclusion remains unchanged: the Vedas are of foreign origin. They would have it both ways: hold on to the fruits of racism but deny that their work has any racist taint!

sponsorship by the ruling authorities in India. Even modern Indologists, while claiming the theory itself to be the result of linguistic research, continue to use arguments that resemble theology more than they do science. In this context, the following remark by the well-known linguist Murray Emeneau quoted earlier bears repeating (in more detail):

> At some time in the second millennium BC, probably comparatively early in the millennium, a band or bands of speakers of an Indo-European language, later to be called Sanskrit, entered India over the northwest passes. *This is our linguistic doctrine which has been held now for more than a century and a half.* There seems to be no reason to distrust the arguments for it, in spite of the traditional Hindu ignorance of any such invasion. (Emeneau 1954: p 282; emphasis added.)

This is not science, but theology pure and simple. There were also other influences like German nationalistic aspirations and British colonial interests, as we shall soon see. German notions about the 'Aryan race' and the 'Aryan nation' formed a particularly potent combination in sustaining the Aryan invasion theory. All these have left their mark on the version of ancient Indian history still found in textbooks. Thus the current version of ancient Indian history built around the Aryan invasion model represents an interesting mix of linguistic conjectures, German nationalism, British colonial interests, missionary propaganda and Biblical beliefs. Science is the only thing missing from it. Let us next look at its modern incarnation.

Beginning about 1921, the discovery of the great Harappan Civilization of the Indus Valley (actually the Sarasvati, but this was not known at the time) posed a challenge to this theory. Archaeologists could find no evidence for any invasion in ancient times. Nonetheless ingenious explanations continued to be offered to somehow account for the existence of the great civilization—the Harappans of the Indus Valley and beyond—going back more than a thousand years before the supposed arrival of the Aryans. The invading Aryans of course were said to be the people who brought both the Sanskrit language and civilization into India.

In the past two to three decades, data from several other sources, notably the discovery of the course of the ancient Sarasvati River described in the *Rigveda,* finally showed the Aryan invasion to be wholly a myth that is contradicted by all scientific data. This was discussed in the last chapter.

Today, as a result of more scientific approaches based on multidisciplinary research by a new generation of scholars, the Aryan invasion theory is finally on its way out as a historical model for ancient India. While the theory may be discredited, its political (and academic) legacy persists both in Indian politics and in Western academia, which is also highly politicized in this struggle for its survival. (See Supplement I.)

In the next few pages, I will present a brief account of the various factors that went into the creation of the Aryan invasion version of history and its final collapse. Later, the book will also provide an alternative model based on the latest ecological, mathematical and metallurgical data, as well as a fresh examination of ancient records—all of which help shed light on the distribution of the languages of Asia and Europe. The decipherment of the Indus script is also examined. All these go to demolish the Aryan invasion theory. Later, an alternative based on close natural and historical connections between India and Southeast Asia will be given. First it is helpful to look at how scholars from different eras saw ancient India.

Changing perceptions

The work of scholars who have studied ancient India presents a fascinating pattern of changing perceptions revealing how each age tends to view the past through ideas and beliefs nearest to its own. As a society emerging only recently from centuries of colonial rule, it is perhaps natural that interpretations of ancient Indian history should still retain many traces of its colonial past. This picture has been further confounded by two factors. First, a nationalistic reaction by native historians in the years shortly before independence continuing into the present; next, and no less significant, the discovery by eighteenth and nineteenth century European scholars of the profound linguistic and other cultural affinities between ancient India and Europe. The latter has resulted in muddying the waters in both history and linguistics. (A third confusing element is anthropology, which we need not go into here.)

As a result of a historical accident, the first European students of India happened to be linguists drawn to the study of Sanskrit stimulated by the discovery of its similarities to classical European languages like Greek, and the linguistic wonders found in the work of ancient Indian grammarians like Panini. For this reason, until recently, ancient Indian history has been dominated by the theories of linguists like Friedrich Max Müller. Further, some of the leading Indologists of the nineteenth century, including Max Müller himself, happened also to be ardent German nationalists who looked to ancient Indian language, culture and tradition as their spiritual wellspring. It was inevitable that these currents of the age in which they lived should have left their mark on their work on ancient Indian history. Their claims therefore should not be accepted at face value, while ignoring the influences that affected them. They were products of their time, living in an age of European colonialism and German nationalism that we cannot ignore.

In this climate of differing even conflicting interests and emotions, an objective approach to Indian history was scarcely to be expected. It was only in this century, especially following the discovery by archaeologists of the great Indus Valley (Harappan) Civilization that the beginnings of a scientific approach to the study of ancient India became possible. In the past three decades, archaeology has been supplemented by data from marine archaeology, satellite photography, metallurgy and mathematics, as well as increasing recognition of the importance of ecological changes in the study of ancient societies like India. The latest entrant to the field is population genetics. It has helped shed new light on the true nature of ancient migrations and populations. As a result there is now a sea change in our perception of ancient India, and an ongoing revolution in research methods that combine the latest scientific techniques with a critical yet constructive use of ancient records.

These scientific data were not available to nineteenth century pioneers like Max Müller who had little beyond comparative linguistics to go by. We must not lose sight this crucial fact: scientific data and techniques from diverse disciplines were unavailable to nineteenth century pioneers. The fact that most of them also lacked the rudiments of a scientific education is also a factor that needs to be kept in mind. (This is still a problem with many Indologists not recognizing that their theories lead to blatant scientific contradictions.) Further, several of these scholars, perhaps even a majority, were no more than amateurs—colonial bureaucrats and Christian missionaries—who as a rule lacked the necessary scholarly background and the objectivity needed to interpret an ancient and alien culture.

Another problem was that many of these nineteenth century scholars were in the pay of the ruling authorities, with Max Müller himself a prime example. This did not allow them the freedom to stray too far from the official line, which could well cost them their jobs. In the circumstances, it was natural that the version of history they created should suffer from biases and inconsistencies. These crucial facts—a weak to non-existent scientific base and the intrusion of political and career interests—must be kept in mind in examining the work of these scholars from the colonial era. It would be a serious mistake to regard their work as examples of detached scholarship. Academic freedom that we now take for granted did not exist a century ago.

Rise and fall of the Aryan invasion[3]

Going back at least to the late sixteenth century, some European visitors to India had been struck by the remarkable affinities, which they found between Sanskrit and European languages. Fillippo Sassetti, a Florentine merchant living in Goa in 1583–88, observed that there was definitely a connection between Sanskrit and European languages. But it was Sir William Jones, a Calcutta judge and the founder of the Asiatic Society who launched the study of comparative linguistics with the following observation.

> The Sanskrit language, whatever be its antiquity, is of wonderful structure; more perfect than Greek, more copious than Latin, and more exquisitely refined than either, yet bearing to both of them a stronger affinity, both in the roots of the verbs and in the forms of grammar, than could possibly have been produced by accident; so strong, indeed, that no philologer could examine them all three without believing them to have sprung from some common source. (Mukherji 1987: pp 88-9)

This famous statement by Jones on February 2, 1786 is still regarded by many historians as the basis for ancient Indian history. A whole approach to ancient history came into existence flowing from the study of Sanskrit and other languages of Europe and Asia. In the circumstances it is no surprise that linguists like Friedrich Max Müller and Albrecht Weber should have formulated a model of ancient Indian history based on their own theories in comparative linguistics. Although he was not its originator, Max Müller was the most influential proponent of this approach to Indian history.

According to this theory, a people called the Aryans, a branch of the Indo-Europeans living originally in Central Asia or Europe, invaded India and overcame the natives, who according to this theory were a 'rabble of aborginal savages'. The theory also claimed that another branch of the

---

[3] For more on the topics discussed in this chapter, see *The Politics of History* by N.S. Rajaram.

same Indo-Europeans migrated to Europe and became the ancestors of the modern Europeans, especially Germans. (German scholars called the Indo Europeans, *Indogermanische*.) This is the famous Aryan invasion theory that is still treated as a historical fact by many historians both in India and the West. According to this theory, these foreign invaders created both the Vedas and the Sanskrit language.

To arrive at a date for the invasion, Max Müller (and others) relied on the only model for ancient history then available in Europe—the Biblical account of Creation. This theory, first postulated by one Bishop Ussher of Ireland, assigned the date 23 October 4004 BC for the creation of the world and about 2400 BC for the Biblical Flood. Based on this Max Müller assigned 1500 BC for the beginning of the Aryan invasion and 1200 BC for the composition of the *Rigveda*—the most important of ancient Indian scriptures. He then sought to find support for these dates in Indian literature also, notably in a ghost story found in the *Kathasaritsagara,* a collection of fables compiled by the 11-th century AD poet Somadeva of Kashmir.

It may seem extraordinary to us that the foundation of what is taught as history should rest on superstition and ghost stories, but it is a matter of record. It should also be noted that the Biblical Creation theory was the only one available at the time in Europe. When Darwin's Theory of Evolution and his *The Origin of Species* appeared in 1859 it was fiercely resisted for several decades. Devout Christians were in the forefront of this resistance to Darwin's theory, which is still the case in parts of America and Europe. As recently as 1890, most schools taught the Biblical account of creation. The fact that the first English language schools in India were run by Christian missionaries was also responsible for the Biblical theory, and its relative the Aryan invasion, being taught long after Darwin's ideas had come to be widely accepted. Indian history was also fitted into the same Biblical framework.

In Max Müller's defense it must be noted that he was not always dogmatic about his dates, later admitting (Varma 1979: p 92): "Whether the Vedic hymns were written in 1000, 1500 or 2000 or 3000 BC, no power on earth will ever determine." Later events have shown this to have been remarkably prophetic. (See Chapter 3 of my book *The Politics of History* for a fuller account.)

This Aryan invasion model created by linguists has had a reign of over a century and half—including over half a century in independent India.

It has been used as the 'official' version of history first by the British and later by Indian educational authorities themselves after independence. At the same time it is important to note that there have always been dissenting scholars—Indian as well as Western—who rejected both the invasion model and its dates for the Vedas. Swami Vivekananda and Sri Aurobindo were emphatic that Aryans and the Vedas were indigenous to India. Even in Europe, such eminent scholars as Hermann Jacobi and Moritz Winternitz refused to subscribe to the idea of the invasion and the foreign origin of the Vedic Civilization. These soon began to find support in science, particularly Vedic astronomy.

In the year 1893, Hermann Jacobi in Germany and Bal Gangadhar Tilak in India working independently of each other showed that there are astronomical references in the *Rigveda* that indicate knowledge of stellar positions as far back as 4000 BC and beyond. Tilak in particular showed that there are profuse references to stellar and planetary positions not only in the Vedas but also in the associated literature like the *Brahmanas* and the *Sutras* showing that the Vedic people must have been established in India long before 4000 BC.

In addition, F.E. Pargiter, probably the foremost Western student of the Puranas, pointed out in 1922 that ancient Indian literature shows no knowledge of any invasion or migration of the Aryans from outside into India while it does record numerous migrations out of India. By then the Aryan invasion theory had become too well entrenched to be dislodged by a few dissenting voices.

The first real jolt to the established theory came from archaeology. Beginning about 1921, the work of British and Indian archaeologists, notably John Marshall, Daya Ram Sahni and Rakhal Das Bannerji revealed the existence of a vast civilization stretching from the borders of Iran to East UP, with a few sites as far south as the Godavari Valley. This is now famous as the Harappan Civilization of the Indus Valley, more properly the Indus-Sarasvati Civlization. We have already described it in some detail. It was found to have been flourishing more than a thousand years before the supposed Aryan invasion in 1500 BC. This brought seriously into question the whole idea of the invading Aryans as bringers of civilization to India.

Faced with this massive contradiction, historians reacted by suggesting that the ruins were due to the destruction of the cities by the invading Aryans. This added a new wrinkle: scholars now claimed that the

Aryan invaders defeated the 'Dravidian' inhabitants of the Indus Valley who were then forced to migrate south. These scholars then sought to find accounts of the episode—of the destruction of this ancient civilization—in the *Rigveda* itself. There are no such accounts, but scholars pulled out a few passages and twisted their meaning and presented it as 'proof'.

But this changes the whole character of the Aryans as bringers of civilization, and the original natives as a 'rabble of aborginal savages'; the invading Aryans now become the barbarians that destroyed the great civilization created by the native people. As a result, despite numerous ingenious attempts at resolving such contradictions, the Aryan invasion theory can be seen to be seriously in conflict with archaeology. This is still the case though some diehard advocates of the invasion idea are trying to reinterpret or even dismiss archaeological findings as irrelevant. Linguistics by itself has proven unequal to the formidable task of reconstructing the history of ancient India even if its theories about ancient languages are basically correct which is itself seriously in doubt.

Recently, problems have also arisen within linguistics itself showing that the assumptions underlying the linguistic model used in the creation of the Aryan invasion might have been too hasty and based on too scanty data. The work of modern linguists like the Indian polymath Satya Swarup Misra and the Hungarian J. Harmatta has highlighted borrowings from Vedic Sanskrit by Uralic languages of Central Asia and Europe even before 5000 BC (Misra 1992). This gives rise to a truly staggering disparity of over 3000 years from the postulated 1500 BC date for the presence of the Aryans in India. Further, Sanskrit and Vedic terms are found in some inscriptions found in West Asia as far away as Anatolia (Asiatic Turkey). Thus the sole basis for the Aryan invasion theory is brought seriously into question by recent findings within linguistics itself.

The most serious blow to the Aryan invasion idea comes however from archaeology and prehistoric ecology, especially the discovery of the course of the ancient Sarasvati river mentioned in the Vedas. It is a vast subject, which I have already discussed it in some detail in the last chapter. The reader at this point may find it helpful to go back and review it.

The verdict of archaeology and geography is clear and unambiguous: the *Rigveda* describes the geography of India as it was before the Sarasvati dried up, when it was still a flourishing river and a vital source. The Indus-Sarasvati Civilization (or the Harappan Civilization), the vast civilization stretching over a million square kilometers was Vedic Aryan. Both the

Aryan invasion and the Aryan-Dravidian conflicts are therefore pure fiction.

Thus, on the basis of evidence from archaeology, mathematics, astronomy and metallurgy it is now clear that the Aryans must have been firmly established in India by 4000 BC at the latest. By then they were already an advanced civilization. The Indus-Sarasvati civilization came *after* the Vedic Age, and was in fact a continuation of it. The Sutra literature, the *Sulbasutras* in particular, provided the technological basis for the material part of it—like cities, harbors, roads, navigation and others without which such a great civilization is impossible. So the Dravidians were part of the Vedic culture and the Aryan-Dravidian conflicts are a modern day myth. Today, as under the British, it is nothing but a tool of politicians used to divide the people. It later went on to acquire a following among scholars with vested interests who saw themselves as successors to colonial interests.

(To all this must now be added the Jha's proposed decipherment of the Indus script. This shows the language of the Harappans to be Vedic Sanskrit. This demolishes the Aryan invasion theory. But the point is, as Supplement I makes clear, even without the decipherment we have enough scientific evidence to refute the Aryan invasion. As discussed later in the book, the decipherment should not be viewed in isolation.)

This means that the Age of the *Rigveda* could well be part of a civilization before the rise of the civilizations of ancient Egypt, Mesopotamia and the Indus Valley. It is now recognized that there existed a prehistoric civilization in Europe that also predated Egypt and Mesopotamia. As discussed in a later chapter, Indian records point to connections between the Vedic people and the people of prehistoric Europe. This may help account for the similarities found between Indian and European languages and mythologies, without the need for any Aryan invasion. (Genetics also points to a movement in the reverse direction—from east to west. But the time scales have to be much longer.)

All this calls for a complete revision of our idea of Mesopotamia as the cradle of civilization. There was an earlier, primordial, mainly spiritual civilization of which the *Rigveda* is a remnant. (*Sic:* To this must be added recent finds of underwater settlements in Gujarat and Tamil Nadu dating to before 7500 BC, which also casts doubt on the validity of Mesopotamia as the cradle of civilization.)

This being the case, who were the Aryas (or Aryans), the people who contributed so greatly to Indian and world civilization? To answer this we need to free ourselves from European stereotypes, go directly to Indian sources and read what the Aryas had to say about themselves.

Arya: race or culture?

The evidence of science now points to two basic conclusions: first, there was no Aryan invasion, and second, the Rigvedic people were already established in India by 4000 BC. How are we then to account for the continued presence of the Aryan invasion version of history found in history books even today? Some of the results presented here are quite recent and it is probably unrealistic to expect history books to reflect the latest findings. But unfortunately, influential Indian historians and educators continue to resist all revisions and hold on to this racist creation—the Aryan invasion theory. Though there is now a tendency to treat the Aryan-Dravidian division as a linguistic phenomenon, its roots are decidedly racial and political, as we shall soon discover.

Speaking of the Aryan invasion theory, it would be an over-simplification to say: "Germans invented it, British used it," but not by much. The concept of the Aryans as a race and the associated idea of the 'Aryan nation' was very much part of the ideology of German nationalism. For reasons known only to themselves, Indian educational authorities have continued to propagate this obsolete fiction that degrades and divides her people. They have allowed their political biases and career interests to take precedence over the education of children. They continue to propagate a version that has no scientific basis and is contradicted by all sources.

Before getting to the role played by German nationalism, it is useful first to take a brief look at what the word Arya does mean. After Hitler and the Nazi atrocities, most people, especially Europeans are understandably reluctant to be reminded of the word. But that was a European crime; Indians had no part in it. The real Aryans have lived in India for thousands of years without committing anything remotely resembling it.[4]

We have already seen that the idea of Aryans as foreigners who invaded India and destroyed the existing Harappan Civilization is a modern European invention that *receives no support whatsoever from*

---

[4]This though doesn't stop the same scholars from charging those who question the Aryan invasion (like this writer) as nationalistic chauvinists! As remarked in a previous note, some Western academics deny racism but want to hold on to the fruits of race-based theories that grew out of German nationalism.

Indian records or science. The same is true of the notion of the Aryans as a race; it finds no support in Indian literature or tradition. The word 'Arya' in Sanskrit means noble and never a race. (There is no satisfactory word in Sanskrit for race.) In fact, the authoritative Sanskrit lexicon (c. 450 AD), the famous *Amarakosha* gives the following definition:

> *mahākula kulīnārya sabhya sajjana sādhavah*
> An Arya is one who hails from a noble family, of gentle behavior and demeanor, good-natured and of righteous conduct

And the great epic *Ramayana* has a singularly eloquent expression describing Rama as:

> *ārya sarva samashcaiva sadaiva priyadarshanah*
> Arya, who worked for the equality of all and was dear to everyone

The *Rigveda* also uses the word Arya something like thirty six times, but never to mean a race. The nearest to a definition that one can find in the *Rigveda* is probably:

> *prajā ārya jyotiragrāh...* (Children of Arya are led by light)
> *RV*, VII. 33.17

The word 'light' should be taken in the spiritual sense to mean enlightenment. The word *Arya,* according to those who originated the term, is to be used to describe those people who observed a code of conduct; people were Aryans or non-Aryans depending on whether or not they followed this code. This is made entirely clear in the *Manudharma Shastra* or the *Manusmriti* according to which (X.43-45):

> But in consequence of the omission of sacred rites, and of their not heeding the sages, the following people of the noble class [*Arya Kshatriyas*] have gradually sunk to the state of servants—the Paundrakas, Chodas, Dravidas, Kambojas, Yavanas, Shakhas, Paradhas, Pahlavas, Chinas, Kiratas and Daradas.

Two points about this list are worth noting: first, their fall from grace—from the Aryan fold—had nothing to do with race, birth or nationality; it was due entirely to their failure to follow certain sacred rites. Second, the list includes people from all parts of India as well as a few neighboring countries like China and Persia (Pahlavas). Kambojas are from West Punjab, Yavanas from Afghanistan and beyond (not necessarily the

Greeks) while Dravidas refers probably to people from the southwest of India and the South. Thus ancient records contradict this modern notion of Aryan-Dravidian racial divide.[5] We have it on the authority of Manu that the Dravidians were also part of the Aryan fold. Interestingly, so were the Chinese. Race never had anything to do with it until the Europeans adopted the ancient word to give expression to their nationalistic and other prejudices.

Conclusion: Aryan, a European obsession, not a problem

The following simple fact helps place the so-called 'Aryan problem' in perspective: in the whole of the *Rigveda,* made up of ten *mandalas* (books) containing over a thousand *suktas* (hymns), the word Arya appears perhaps some forty times. It may appear as many times in a few pages of a modern European work, most infamously in Hitler's *Mein Kampf.* So any modern work on the Aryan problem can only be a commentary on this vast nineteenth and twentieth century Euroepan literature having little to do with ancient India.

In summary, one may safely say that the word Arya denoted certain spiritual and humanistic values that defined an ancient civilization. The entire Aryan civilization—the civilization of Vedic India and what succeeded it (including the Dravidian)—was driven and sustained by this ideal. The whole of ancient Indian literature: from the Vedas, the Brahmanas to the Puranas to the epics like the *Mahabharata* and the *Ramayana* can be seen as a record of the struggles of an ancient people striving to live up to the ideal. Anyone regardless of birth, race or national origin could become Aryan by following this code of conduct. It was not something to be imposed upon others by the sword or by proselytization. Viewed in this light, the whole notion of any 'Aryan invasion' is an absurdity. It is like talking about 'invasion of scientific thinking'.

It is undeniable that the concept of the Aryan race and the Aryan-Dravidian divide is a modern European invention that receives no support from any Indian source. (See Supplement I for a summary.) To apply it to a people who lived thousands of years ago is an exercise in anachronism. It was a political creation to understand which we need to look at the politics behind it. This is what we do next.

---

[5]There is no word for race in any Indian language. Further, adoption was allowed in India even by kings. This rules out any concept of racial identity.

4.

History and politics: Scholars and patrons

Background: German nationalists and British masters

This being the situation, how are we account for the continued presence in history books of the version of history based on the Aryan invasion for more than a century? First point to note is that most nineteenth century European Indologists knew no science at all; this we have seen in the case of Max Müller—the greatest of them—with his Biblical superstitions. There was a more fundamental reason: it was never the real intent of colonial authorities and interested scholars to discover the truth about ancient history. They were not research scholars being paid to make discoveries about India's past. Their interest lay in using whatever material they could find, and put it to best possible use to serve their own political, commercial and missionary ends. In other words, British authorities were simply making their job of ruling Indians easy by subverting Indian history and tradition. This is only to be expected.

By a strange twist of fate, the influence of German nationalism with its baggage of race theories also entered the picture. In the light of all this, it is safe to say that it was influenced more by European political, religious and economic considerations than what science or Indian records had to say. That is to say, the Aryan invasion of history owes more to European political currents than Indian sources.

As a result, before examining what science has to tell us about ancient India, it is revealing to take a look at how large a role was played by the ruling political interests in the creation of a version of history that continues to be taught in schools. This is a fascinating story, which we can only touch upon here. (See my book *The Politics of History* for a more detailed discussion.)[1]

---

[1]*The Invasion That Never Was* by Michel Danino is also recommended.

European currents: 'Aryan nation'

In order to understand the European misuse of the word Arya as a race, and the creation of the Aryan invasion idea, we need to go back to eighteenth and nineteenth century Europe, especially to Germany. The idea has its roots in European anti-Semitism. Recent research by scholars like Poliakov, Shaffer and others has shown that the idea of the invading Aryan race can be traced to eighteenth and nineteenth century Europeans to give themselves an identity that was free from the taint of Judaism. The Bible consists of two books: the Old Testament and the New Testament. The Old Testament gives the traditional history of mankind. It is of course a Jewish creation. The New Testament is also of Jewish origin, but was later turned against the Judaism of its founding fathers. In fact, anti-Semitism first makes its appearance in the New Testament, including in the Gospels. Nonetheless, without Judaism there would be no Christianity.

To free themselves from this Jewish heritage, some intellectuals of Christian Europe looked east, to Asia. There they saw two ancient civilizations—India and China. To them the Indian Aryans were preferable as ancestors to the Chinese. Shaffer observed:

> Many scholars such as Kant and Herder, began to draw analogies between the myths and philosophies of ancient India and the West. In their attempt to separate Western European culture from its Judaic heritage, many scholars were convinced that the origin of Western culture was to be found in India rather than in the ancient Near East. (Shaffer 1984: p 80)

So they became Aryans. However, it was not the whole human race that was given this Aryan ancestry, but only a white race that came down from the mountains of Asia, subsequently became Christian and colonized Europe. No less an intellectual than Voltaire claimed to be "convinced that everything has come down to us from the banks of the Ganges—astronomy, astrology, metempsychosis, etc." (But Voltaire was emphatically not intolerant; he was in fact a strong critic of the Church of his day.)

A student today can scarcely have an idea of the extraordinary influence of race theories in eighteenth and nineteenth century Europe. Many educated people truly believed that human qualities could be predicted on the basis of measurements of physical characteristics like eye color, length of the nose (called 'nasal index') and such. It went beyond prejudice: it was a belief system amounting to ideology. It was the basis not only of German nationalism but also much of European imperialism under the name of the 'White Man's Burden.'

Modern scholars are loathe to be reminded of this sordid past, but here is an example of what passed for informed discussion on 'race science.' It is by the well-known French savant Paul Topinard. Much of the discourse centered on the relative merits of racial types called dolichocephalics and brachycephalics, though no one seemed to have a clear idea of what was which. Here is what Topinard wrote in 1893. It should give modern readers an idea of the level of scientific thinking prevailing in those days:

> The Gauls, according to history, were a people formed of two elements: the leaders or conquerors, blond, tall dolichocephalic, leptroscopes, etc. But the mass of the people, were small, relatively brachycephalic chaemeophrosopes. The brachycephalics were always oppressed. They were the victims of dolicocephalics who carried them off from their fields. ... The blond people changed from warriors into merchants and industrial workers. The brachycephalics breathed again. Being naturally prolific, their numbers [of brachycephalics] increased while the dolichocephalics naturally diminished. ... Does the future not belong to them? [*Sic:* Belong to whom? – dolichocephalic leptroscopes, or brachycephalic chaemeophrosopes?][2]

This tongue-twisting passage may seem bizarre to a modern reader, but it was considered an erudite piece of reasoning when it was written. In its influence and scientific unsoundness and dogmatism, it can only be compared in this century to Marxism and Fascism. The emergence of molecular genetics has shown these race theories to be completely false. In fact, the most recent work in human genetics shows that the concept of race itself has no scientific basis. Studies have shown that genetic variations within a particular human group are much greater than variations between different groups. (More of this later.) As far back as 1938, the great biologist Julian Huxley denounced the idea of the 'Aryan race' as "demonstrably false." But British authorities and German nationalists continued using it anyway because it served their political purpose.

---

[2]This and other interesting and hard to find passages can be found in the special issue of *Manthan* (April-September 1994) on Genesis of the Aryan Myth, published by Deen Dayal Research Institute, New Delhi. The passage cited above is on page 51.

Here is the truth: by creating this pseudo-science based on race, Europeans of the Age of Enlightenment sought to free themselves from their Jewish heritage. It is interesting to note that this very same theory—of the Aryan invasion and colonization of Europe—was later applied to India and became the Aryan invasion theory of India. In reality it was nothing more than a projection into the remote past of the contemporary European experience in colonizing parts of Asia and Africa. Substituting European for Aryan, and Asian or African for Dravidian will give us a description of any of the innumerable colonial campaigns in the eighteenth and the nineteenth century. According to this theory, the Aryans were carbon copies of colonizing Europeans. Seen in this light the theory is not even especially original.

The greatest effect of these ideas was on the psyche of the German people. German nationalism was probably the most momentous political movement of nineteenth century Europe. The idea of the Aryans as a superior race played a major role in German unification. We now see Germany as a rich and powerful country, but the German people at the beginning of the nineteenth century were weak and divided. There was no German nation at the time. The map of Europe was dotted with numerous petty German principalities and dukedoms that had always been at the mercy of the neighboring great powers—Austria and France. For more than two centuries, from the time of the Thirty Years War to the Napoleonic conquests, armies had marched through these powerless German states treating these people and their rulers with utter disdain. It was very much in the interests of the French to keep the German people divided, a tactic applied also to India by the British. Every German at the time believed that he and his rulers were little more than pawns in great power rivalries. This had built up deep resentments in the hearts and minds of the German people. It was to have catastrophic consequences for history.

In this climate of alienation and impotence, it is not surprising that German intellectuals should have sought solace in the culture of an ancient exotic land like India. Some of us can recall a similar sentiment among Americans during the era of Vietnam and the Cold War, with many of them taking interest in Eastern religions and philosophy. These German intellectuals also felt a kinship towards India as a people subjugated like themselves. Some of the great German thinkers of the era—Humbolt, Frederick and Wilhem Schlegel, Schopenhauer and many others were students of Indian literature and philosophy. Hegel, the greatest philosopher of the age and a major influence on German nationalism was fond of saying that in philosophy and literature, Germans were the pupils of Indian sages. Humbolt went so far as to declare in 1827: "The *Bhagavadgita* is perhaps the loftiest and the deepest thing that the world has to show." This was the general climate in Germany when it was feeling the rising tide of nationalism.

German involvement in Indian history and tradition was emotional and romantic; the British outlook however was largely practical, even though there were scholars like Jones and Colebrooke who were admirers of India and its literature. Well before the 1857 uprising it was recognized that the British rule in India could not be sustained without a large number of Indian collaborators. Faced with this reality, influential Englishmen like Thomas Babbington Macaulay, Chairman of the Education Board, sought to set up an educational system modeled along British lines that would also serve to undermine the Hindu tradition. While not a missionary himself, Macaulay came from a deeply religious family steeped in the Protestant Christian faith. His father was a Presbyterian minister and his mother a Quaker. His interest in converting the Hindus had also a practical motive. He believed that the conversion of Hindus to Christianity held the answer to the problems of administering India. His idea was to create an English educated elite that would repudiate its tradition and become British collaborators. In 1836, while serving as chairman of the Education Board in India, he enthusiastically wrote his father:

> Our English schools are flourishing wonderfully. The effect of this education on the Hindus is prodigious. ...It is my belief that if our plans of education are followed up, there will not be a single idolator among the respectable classes in Bengal thirty years hence. And this will be effected without any efforts to proselytise, without the smallest interference with religious liberty, by natural operation of knowledge and reflection. I heartily rejoice in the project. (See *Vedic Aryans and the Origins of Civilization* by Rajaram and Frawley, p 31.)

So religious conversion and colonialism were to go hand in hand. As Arun Shourie has brought to light in his *Missionaries in India,* Christian missions formed an appendage of the colonial government by working hand in glove with the government. In a real sense, they cannot be called religious organizations at all but an unofficial arm of the Imperial Administration. (The same is true of many Christian missions in Central

American countries who were, and probably are, in the pay of American government organizations.)

The key point in all this is Macaulay's belief that 'knowledge and reflection' on the part of the Hindus, especially the Brahmins, would cause them to give up their age old beliefs in favor of Christianity. In effect, his idea was to turn the strength of Hindu intellectuals against them, by exploiting their commitment to scholarship and uproot their own tradition. Specifically, his plan was to educate the Hindus to become Christians and turn them into collaborators more loyal to their new masters than to their own culture and tradition. One may think he was being naive to believe that his scheme could really succeed in converting India to Christianity. At the same time it is a measure of his seriousness that Macaulay persisted with the idea for fifteen years until he found the money and the right man for turning his utopian idea into reality.

Baron Bunsen, Max Müller's patron

F. Max Müller

Max Müller's 'bargain with the devil'[3]

In pursuit of his goal Macaulay needed someone who would translate and interpret Indian scriptures, especially the Vedas, in such a way that the newly educated Indian elite would see the differences between them and

[3]Details can be found in *The Politics of History* and also *Vedic Aryans and the Origins of Civilization.*

the Bible and choose the latter. Upon his return to England, after a good deal of effort he found a talented but impoverished young German Sanskrit scholar by name Friedrich Max Müller who was willing to undertake this arduous task. In this he was helped by the Prussian ambassador in England, Baron von Bunsen, who had known Max Müller from his early youth. Though Macaulay is invariably given the credit for Max Müller's career, it was Bunsen who had groomed the young and somewhat unsophisticated Max Müller to be acceptable to the English ruling class of which Lord Macaulay was an influential member. Bunsen, who had pretensions to being an oriental scholar, deserves as much credit as Macaulay for Max Müller's spectacular career that was to follow. He introduced Max Müller to Macaulay on Christmas Day of 1854.

After some initial difficulty, Macaulay used his influence with the East India Company to provide funds for Max Müller's translation of the *Rigveda*. Though an ardent German nationalist, Max Müller agreed for the sake of Christianity to work for the East India Company, which in reality meant the British Government of India. He also badly needed a major sponsor for his ambitious plans. With Macaulay's support, obtained through Bunsen's influence, he had at last found one.

This was the genesis of his great enterprise, publishing the *Rigveda* with Sayana's commentary and the editing of the *Sacred Books of the East.* There can be no doubt at all regarding Max Müller's commitment to the conversion of Indians to Christianity. Writing to his wife in 1866, he observed:

> It [the *Rigveda*] is the root of their religion and to show them what the root is, I feel sure, is the only way of uprooting all that has sprung from it during the last three thousand years. (See *Vedic Aryans and the Origins of Civilization,* op.cit, pp 33–4.)

Two years later he also wrote the Duke of Argyle, then (acting) Secretary of State for India: "The ancient religion of India is doomed. And if Christianity does not take its place, whose fault will it be?" The facts therefore are clear: like Lawrence of Arabia later, Max Müller, though a scholar, was an agent of the British government paid to advance its colonial interests.

But he remained an ardent German nationalist even while working in England. This helps explain why he used his position as a recognized Vedic and Sanskrit scholar to promote the idea of the 'Aryan race' and the

'Aryan nation', both favorite slogans of German nationalists. Though he was later to repudiate it, it was Max Müller as much as anyone who popularized the notion of Arya as a race. This of course was to reach its culmination in the rise of Hitler and the horrors of Nazism in our own century.

It would of course be unfair to blame Max Müller for the horrors of Nazism, but he, as an eminent scholar of the Vedas and Sanskrit, bears a heavy responsibility for the deliberate misuse of a term in response to the emotion of the moment. He was guilty of giving scriptural sanction to the worst prejudice of his or any age. Not everyone however was guilty of such abuse; Wilhem Schlegel, no less a German nationalist, or romantic, always used the word 'Arya' to mean honorable and never in a racial sense. Max Müller's misuse of the term may be pardonable in an ignoramus, but not in a scholar of his stature.

At the same time it is fair to point out that there is nothing to indicate that Max Müller was himself a racist. He was a decent and honorable man who had many Indian friends. He simply allowed himself to be carried away by the emotion of the moment, and the heady feeling of being regarded an Aryan sage by fellow German nationalists. To be always in the public eye was a lifelong weakness with the man. With the benefit of hindsight we may say that Max Müller saw the opportunity and made a 'bargain with the devil' to gain fame and fortune. It would be a serious error, however, to judge the man based on this one unseemly episode in a many sided life. His contribution as editor and publisher of ancient works—if not as a scholar—is great beyond dispute. For all his faults—opportunism and unsound scholarship in particular, he was a great man.

Max Müller's flip-flop: from race to language

Much is now made of Max Müller's later repudiation of the racial aspects of the Aryan theory, claiming it to be a linguistic concept. But this again owed more to winds of change in European politics than to science or scholarship. Britain was watching the progress of German nationalism with rising anxiety that burst into near hysteria when Prussia crushed France in the Franco-Prussian war in 1871. This led to German unification under the banner of Prussia. Suddenly Germany became the most populous and powerful country in Western Europe and the greatest threat to British ambitions. Belief was widespread among British Indian authorities that India and Sanskrit studies had made a major contribution to German unification. Sir Henry Maine, a former Vice Chancellor of Calcutta University and an advisor to the Viceroy, echoed the sentiment of many influential Englishmen when he said: "A nation has been born out of Sanskrit." (*The Politics of History,* op. cit.)

This was a wild exaggeration, but to the British still reeling from the 1857 revolt, the specter of German unification being repeated in India seemed very real. Max Müller though found himself in a tight spot. Though a German by birth, he was now comfortably established in England, in the middle of his lifework on the Vedas and the *Sacred Books of the East.* His youthful flirtation with German nationalism and Aryan race theories could now cost him dear. German unification was followed in England by an outburst of British jingoism in which Bismarck and his policies were being daily denounced; Bismarck had become extremely unpopular in England for his expansionist policies. With his background as a German nationalist, the last thing Max Müller could afford was to be seen as advocating German ideology in Victorian England. He had no choice but to repudiate his former theories simply to survive in England. He reacted by hastily propounding a new 'linguistic theory' of the Aryan invasion.

So in 1872, immediately following German unification, the culmination of the century long dream of German nationalists, Friedrich Max Müller marched into a university in German occupied France (Strasbourg) and dramatically denounced the German doctrine of the Aryan race. He now began to insist that by Aryan he meant language and never a race! But his past position kept dogging him, and politicians and propagandists kept on citing him as authority for their race theories. Finally he lost all patience and burst out in 1888:

> I have declared again and again that if I say Aryan, I mean neither blood nor bones, nor skull nor hair; *I mean simply those who speak the Aryan language.* ...To me an ethnologist who speaks of Aryan blood, Aryan race, Aryan eyes and hair is as great a sinner as a linguist who speaks of a dolicocephalic dictionary or of brachycephalic grammar. (V*vedic Aryans...* op.cit. p36; emphasis added.)

"Methinks the lady doth protest too much," said Shakespeare, about a woman's excessive show of grief following her husband's murder. The same may be said of Max Müller. From that point on, just as he had been an upholder of the Aryan race theory for the first twenty years of his career, he was to remain its staunch opponent for the remaining thirty years of his life. It is primarily in the second role that he is remembered today, except by those familiar with the whole history.

Let us now take a final look at this famous (or infamous) theory. It was first an Aryan invasion theory of Europe created by Europeans to free themselves from the Jewish heritage of Christianity. This later led to Hitler and Nazism. The theory was transferred to India and got mixed up with the study of Sanskrit and European languages. Europeans (or people of the Eurasian steppes), now called Indo-Europeans, became the invading Aryans and the natives became Dravidians. British hired Max Müller to use this theory to turn the Vedas into an inferior scripture, to help turn educated Hindus into Christian collaborators. Max Müller used his position as a Vedic scholar to boost German nationalism by giving scriptural sanction to the German idea of the Aryan race. Following German unification under Bismarck, British public and politicians became scared and anti-German. At this, Max Müller, worried about his position in England got cold feet, and saved himself by denouncing his own former racial theory and turned it into a linguistic theory. In all this, where was the science?

Neo-racism in the garb of genetics[4]

Racism is now an ugly word. Most countries of the world have outlawed it. Academics, Western academics in particular, are highly sensitive to any suggestion that they might be holding racist views. This is the reason that Indo-European studies stress that language and culture rather than race (which has no scientific basis) are the foundation of their discipline. (This too may be seen as a case of the lady protesting too much.) This was not true in the first half of the 20th century, especially before Hitler and the Nazi holocaust brought the whole of "race science" into disrepute. Race, including the so-called Aryan race, though denounced by scientists like Huxley was very much part of the academic discourse in anthropology and history.

This does not mean that racist ideas have altogether disappeared from people's minds, especially in the West. Like the repackaging of the discredited Aryan Invasion Theory (AIT) as the Aryan Migration Theory (AMT)—and now as Aryan Influx Theory (AIT again), some writers are

---

[4]The next couple of sections contain some technical material (which I have greatly simplified). I suggest that the reader bear with it because of its importance.

advancing the scientifically discredited notion of race in new garb as genetic markers. This should be examined and put in its proper place. This is what I propose to do next. We need also to understand how race made its insidious appearance under colonial patronage in the guise of anthropology.

In the past few years, there have been several articles purporting to show that the Indian caste system was imposed by invading (or migrating) Indo-Europeans—or 'Aryans'—though the term Arya has lost some of its appeal following Hitler. This is claimed to have scientific support in the form of genetic evidence of the present day Indian population. In an article entitled "Genetic Evidence on the Origins of Indian Caste Populations," eighteen authors, mainly from Utah in the U.S. and Vishakapatnam in India, led by Michael Bamshad of the Department of Pediatrics from the University of Utah make the claim that there were several waves of immigration into India, the last of which (from Europe) was responsible for the caste system. In their words:

> In the most recent of these waves [of immigration], Indo-European speaking people from West Eurasia entered India from the Northwest and diffused throughout the subcontinent. They purportedly admixed with or displaced Dravidic-speaking populations. Subsequently, they may have established the Hindu caste system and placed themselves in castes of higher rank. (See Bamshad, et al, in the Bibliography.)

To begin with it is patently absurd to mix genetics and language: how does one distinguish the genes of "Dravidic-speaking populations" from those of "Indo-European speakers?" Never mind also that no such language as 'Indo-European' has ever been found. The next point to note is that it is impossible to trace the origin of a segment of a population like upper caste Indians through genetic analysis: the genetic variation within any group—like the upper castes—is always greater than the variation between two groups like the upper caste Indians and Europeans. Scientifically speaking it requires no great effort to demolish the claim. This can be seen by looking at the Zoroastrian Parsees, who emigrated from Persia only some 1200 years ago.

This of course, we know from historical records. But Bamshad and his colleagues would have us believe that they can detect this from genetic analysis, and even "unequivocally demonstrate" it—as Bamshad put it in a press statement, going beyond what he claimed in his article. This means his genetic analysis should be able to tell us how the Parsees living in

Western India happen to be speaking Gujarati. To go by the Aryan invasion analogy, the migrating (or invading) Parsees brought the ancestor of the Gujarati language and imposed it on the native population, which the Bamshad method can "unequivocally demonstrate" with the help of genetic analysis![5]

(As an aside, from the fact that the Parsees of India happen to speak Gujarati, we can also create a Parsee Invasion Theory or PIT that postulates that the Gujarati language and culture came to India with the invading Parsees!)

A point to note is that despite its appeal to science, it is simply a repackaging of nineteenth century colonial race prejudice and propaganda. No less a 'scholar' than Max Müller wrote: "...how the [English] descendants of the same [Aryan] race, to which the first conquerors and masters of India belonged, return ...to accomplish the glorious work of civilization, which had been left unfinished by their Aryan brethren."[6]

There was more than scholarship involved in this. We have already seen that Max Müller was as much a colonial-missionary political agent as he was a scholar, for which he was of course richly rewarded. As he proudly declared in his *Autobiography:* "Lord Derby, then Secretary of State for India, declared that the scholars who had discovered and proved the close relationship between Sanskrit and English, had rendered more valuable service to the [British] Government of India than many a regiment." The most eloquent statement relating this 'history' to the British rule came from Stanley Baldwin (several times prime minister), in a speech he made in the House of Commons in 1929:

> Ages and ages ago, there sat, side by side, the ancestors of the English, Rajputs and Brahmins [upper caste Indians]. Now, after ages, ...the two branches of the great Aryan ancestry have again been brought together by Providence.... By establishing British rule in India, God said to the British, "I have brought you and the Indians together after a long separation, not in order that you should lord over them, or that you should exploit them, but in order that should recognize your kinship with them.... It is your duty to raise

---

[5]Bamshad is said to have changed his stand and no longer claims a genetic basis for caste. But the details of his retraction, if that, are still unclear. Also, it doesn't matter since it is easily refuted by science.

[6]A useful reference is *The Invasion that Never Was* by Michel Danino in the Bibliography. It does not however discuss more recent findings from natural history and genetics.

> them to their own level as quickly as possible, and work together; brothers as you are, for the evolution of humanity…." (Danino, op. cit.)

One can again detect the lady protesting too much in the homily (put in God's mouth): "I have brought you and the Indians together… not in order that you should lord over them, or you should exploit them…" That though was exactly what the British did in the name of God!

From brotherhood, it took only a step to turn them into oppressors. This was done with a sleight of hand by missionary 'scholars' and colonial officials. Anthropologists like Herbert Risley, a colonial official, equated caste with race with the help of what he and his colleagues claimed were measurements of facial features, of the nose in particular. Risley wrote in 1891: "The social position of a caste varies inversely as its nasal index…. Community of race… is the real meaning of the caste system."

So according to race 'scientist' Risley, longer the nose, higher the caste!

All this 'science' was part of the agenda to divide the people of India into antagonistic groups under labels like Aryan and Dravidian to facilitate colonial rule and conversion to Christianity. The most influential figure in this was Robert Caldwell, Bishop of Tirunelveli, the author of *Comparative Grammar of the Dravidian or South Indian Family of Languages*. First published in 1856, it continues its influence today, especially in Tamil Nadu. This is due less to its scholarly content than the fact that it became the political manifesto of Dravidian politicians who not infrequently engaged in outrageously crude conduct towards innocent people that they labeled as descendants of Aryan oppressors.

A study that appeared in February 2004 takes this exercise further by claiming (following Bamshad) that tribal females and caste females are of indigenous origin while caste males are descended from Eurasian ancestors. Further, they claim that this is supported by linguistic and archaeological evidence. Upon closer examination, one finds no evidence but a circular argument that proves itself by repetition. It is nothing but a combination of ignorance and shoddy science.

It is worth noting that one of the co-authors repudiated the claims. For example, Bamshad's label of Europe had been applied to "anything West of the Indus," and his sample was from the East Coast of India! Further, claims were made about the genetic origin of Indo-European language speakers, who, needless to say, are not distinguished by genetic features.

(I commented on it earlier.) Further, there is the claim that these Eurasian (Aryans)—that too males only—arrived in India 3500 years ago (1500 BC). There is no genetic method of determining this date; Max Müller derived the 1500 BC date for the Aryan invasion based on the Biblical belief that the world was created on 23 October 4004 BC!

So science plus linguistics equals Biblical superstition!

In evaluating all this, it helps to recall Risley's claim, "Community of race… is the real meaning of the caste system." We are asked to believe that theories about racial invasions and migrations, concocted by nineteenth century colonial officials like Risley and missionary propagandists like Bishop Caldwell—and modern Dravidian politicians—has all been proved by the magic of genetic research!

Corrections

Happily, some recent studies led by the distinguished human geneticist Cavalli-Sforza and his colleagues, have taken steps to correct this error. An important article based on a study of Indian tribal and caste populations by Cavalli-Sforza and his colleagues observes:[7]

> Taken together, these results show that Indian tribal and caste populations derive largely from the same genetic heritage of Pleistocene southern and western Asians *and have received limited gene flow from external regions since the Holocene.* The phylogeography [neighboring branches] of the primal mtDNA and Y-chromosome founders suggests that these southern Asian Pleistocene coastal settlers from Africa would have provided the inocula for the subsequent differentiation of the distinctive eastern and western Eurasian gene pools. (Italics added.)

Put in non-technical language, it means that the Indian population—upper castes, tribals (or indigenous peoples), Dravidians and so forth—are mainly of indigenous origin, and the contribution of immigrants (gene flow) is negligible. This is a major blow to the many invasion-migration theories that continue to dominate academic (and political) discourse in India (and in Indo-European studies in the West). These of course hold that only the *adivasis* ('first settlers') as tribals are often called, are indigenous while caste Hindus are descended from later immigrants, with the upper castes made up of immigrants from Europe. What these careful scientific studies have shown is this is simply not true.

---

[7]See the article by Kisivild, …Cavalli-Sforza et. al., in the Bibliography.

A basic fallacy in many of these analyses is to compare paternal lineages using Y-chromosomes and maternal lineages using mitochondrial DNA (mtDNA). (Y-chromosomes are passed on along the male line while the mtDNA are transmitted along the female line.) The mtDNA mutate (change) much more rapidly than other DNA (or nuclear DNA)—by as much as *15 to 20 times.* The Y-chromosomes on the other hand hardly change at all. As Walter Bodmer, one of the originators of the Human Genome Project observed:

> No matter where they look, scientists have found that the Y chromosome, regardless of race or creed, has a molecular configuration that hardly varies at all. It does not matter whether the sample is Japanese, or from a Bushman, or a South American Indian, its composition produces extraordinarily few distinctive characteristics and *none that can distinguish human populations from each other...* (Emphais added.)

This digression is necessary to expose the sources and motivations that lurk behind the 'research' of men like Michael Bamshad who would seek to prove all this with the help of genetics. Since many of us have a tendency to accept as true whatever is presented as a scientific finding, it is necessary to take a critical attitude whenever a scientifically discredited notion like race is repackaged as a new scientific discovery.[8]

The sum total of all this: the Aryan invasion theory is dead. Repackaging it as genetic research will not revive the corpse. (It is now known that the genetic evidence in fact shows that *all non-African humans in the world today are of South Asian origin.*

Who were the Dravidians?

The question next is who really are the Dravidians? As far as Indian sources go Dravida is simply a geographical term describing roughly the geographical south or Peninsular India. Traditionally, the *panca dravida* Brahmins are—Gurjara, Maharashtra, Karnata, Andhra and Dravida. These refer to the people living (roughly) in the present day states of Gujarat, Maharashtra, Karnataka, Andhra Pradesh and Tamil Nadu (and Kerala). That is to say it is strictly a geographical designation but with some overlapping of language and culture.

---

[8]Though not gemane here, it is a scientific fact that biological connections between India and Southeast Asia are much closer than with Central Asia or Europe. This extends to climate, flora and fauna, and people, as well as culture. It is also more ancient.

The idea of dividing the people of the 'Dravidian' south by pitting them against the 'oppressive' Aryans of the north was a missionary tactic. As previously noted, the most influential figure in this was Robert Caldwell, Bishop of Tirunelveli, who wrote the highly influential *Comparative Grammar of the Dravidian or South Indian Family of Languages*. His theory claimed that Dravidians were Scythians who brought a Scythian language which later became Dravidian. In effect it was a double invasion theory—a Scythio-Dravidian invasion followed by the invading Aryans.

As with everything else that originated in the colonial period, it was rooted in politics rather than scholarship. It was part of the missionary-colonial agenda to divide the people of India into antagonistic groups under labels like Aryan and Dravidian to facilitate colonial rule and conversion to Christianity. Caldwell himself admitted it. When another scholar (Gover) criticized Caldwell for his unsound theories about the Scythian family and Dravidian languages, it drew the following response: "It would have been well, if Mr. Gover had made himself sure of perfectly apprehending Dr. Caldwell's Scythic theory before regarding its refutation ... as not only of considerable moment from a philological point of view *but of vast moral and political importance.*"

Needless to say, by 'moral and political' Caldwell (writing in third person) meant Christian missionary and British colonial interests. First published in 1856, Caldwell's book continues its influence today, especially in Tamil Nadu. This is due less to its scholarly content than the fact that it became the political manifesto of Dravidian politicians. Essentially it was part of caste-based politics that has dominated Tamil Nadu.

This too has missionary roots. Christian propagandists like Caldwell were unhappy that they could get converts only from the lower strata of Hindu society. Regardless of internal divisions, all segments of Hindu society—and many Muslims as well—looked to the Brahmins for moral and intellectual guidance. Caldwell and his fellow missionaries saw Brahmins as the greatest obstacle to their program. So they attacked Brahmins in the most venomous language as oppressors of society. This is still the case. The idea was to turn the people against those who were seen as preservers and perpetuators of Hindu culture and tradition.

This idea of dividing a conquered people and creating antagonisms was standard missionary tactic, which later was exploited in the name of 'race science' by colonial governments. It was by no means limited to India. Divide and convert preceded divide and rule everywhere the Europeans went. Much of the bloodletting in ethnic conflicts in Africa today is due to such artificial divisions created by the missionaries.

This may be seen in the recent Hutu-Tutsi conflicts in Rwanda and its neighboring countries where it has been particularly virulent. It was propaganda of European missionaries, academics and French colonial officials that gave rise to the idea that the Hutus and the Tutsis were physically different, and that the Tutsis were a superior race, which had conquered the region and enslaved the Hutus. This historical fallacy, which was the result of racist European concepts being applied to an African reality, was what made the Hutus react against the Tutsis, resulting in civili conflict and boodletting on a massive scale.

The Aryan-Dravidian divide is simply another example of this colonial-missionary brainwashing. This has continued to the present largely because humanities education in India (and other countries) is still dominated by Christian institutions of the colonial era.

Scholars as courtiers: Max Müller and his tribe

By a strange turn of fate, the Aryan theory and its political influence reappeared in independent India in the guise of North against South divide that dominated Dravidian politics for over half a century. Just as Max Müller (and a few others) found prestige and patronage by serving British politicians, a new breed of scholars has found it profitable to serve the 'Dravidian' political cause and its advocates. This is a little-known chapter in Indian historical scholarship. Let us take a final look at Max Müller before we turn to other things.

Max Müller is a forgotten figure today, except in India. Though no one in Germany today has heard of him, the German Government shrewdly uses his name in India for its cultural institutions. They know that educated Indians revere his memory though Germans in his time despised him as a traitor and a turncoat who turned against the Aryan race theory to save himself in England. They felt he sold out to the British for the sake of his career. He is not remembered well in England either, if remembered at all. The classic 1911 edition of the *Encyclopedia Britannica* describes him in the following words:

> Though undoubtedly a great scholar, Max Müller did not so much represent scholarship pure and simple as her hybrid types—the scholar-author and the

> scholar-courtier. In the former capacity, though manifesting little of the originality of genius, he endered [*Sic:* rendered] vast service by popularizing high truths among high minds [and among the highly placed]. ...There were drawbacks in both respects: the author was too prone to build on insecure foundations, and the man of the world incurred censure for failings which may perhaps be best indicated by the remark that he seemed too much of a diplomatist.

His contemporaries were less charitable. They charged that Max Müller had an eye "only for crowned heads." His acquaintances included a large number of princes and potentates—with little claim to scholarship—and a maharaja or two thrown in.[9]

Even today, Max Müller's line is far from extinct. But where he went on to cultivate the likes of Prince Albert of Saxe-Coburg-Gotha (Queen Victoria's husband and a fellow German), his successors today have to make do with the patronage of sundry Indian politicians. Dravidian politics, fathered by Christian missionaries like Bishop Caldwell, came to dominate Tamil Nadu politics soon after independence. It was blatantly casteist, but its leaders felt it would be useful to have some scholars supporting their claims that South India—Tamil Nadu in particular—had been victimized by the invading Aryans. This of course would be their political slogan—the one they would use to tell the people that they would correct past injustices.

With this in view, they looked around for an academic or two to give their political theme some respectability. This became fertile ground for a few Western Indologists who found opportunities shrinking following the end of the British rule. Like the Aryan theories, this Dravidianism has its unseemly side, with prejudice and sectarianism rearing its ugly head in what should be a strictly academic debate.

One of the strongest advocates of Dravidians as the creators of the Harappan civilization and some form of Dravidian as the language of the Indus seals is the Finnish anthropologist Asko Parpola. What is remarkable is the manner in which he and his supporters have attacked those (like N. Jha) who have taken a different approach. In the recently published *Lost Languages: The Enigma of The World's Undeciphered Scripts,* Andrew Robinson drawing upon Parpola attacks Jha's

[9]This too was not without profit, for the Raja of Venkatagiri financed publication of the second edition of his *Rigveda.* Contrary to common belief, he did not translate the Vedas except for a handful of hymns.

decipherment as:[10] "an unashamedly nationalistic 'decipherment' by a North Indian."

In other words, Jha's work should be rejected not on scholarly grounds but because he is a North Indian! This is not far removed from the position taken by some 'scientists' in Nazi Germany who rejected Einstein's Theory of Relativity because its creator was a Jew. This should give an idea of how far removed 'scholarship' is from objectivity even today. As we shall see later in the book, Jha's work represents a major landmark that demolishes the work of Parpola and several other political scholars. Recognition of this fact probably accounts for the extraordinary language against a truly great scholar like N. Jha.

Path of science

The fact that Europeans, especially Germans with their newfound nationalism, should have concocted this race-based scenario, which, by repeated assertion became a belief system, is not to be wondered at. They were trying to give themselves a cultural identity, entirely understandable in a people as deeply concerned about their history and origins as the modern Europeans. But how are we to account for the tenacious attachment to this fiction that is more propaganda than history on the part of 'establishment' Indian historians? It is not greatly to their credit that modern Indian historians—with rare exceptions—have failed to show the independence of mind necessary to subject this theory to a fresh examination and come up with a more realistic version of history. Probably they lack the necessary scientific skills and have little choice beyond continuing along the same well-worn paths that don't demand much more than reiterating nineteenth century formulations.

We no longer have to continue along this discredited path. Now thanks to science, especially the pioneering exploration of V.S. Wakankar and his discovery of the Vedic Sarasvati River, followed by Jha's work on the Indus (Harappan) script and related topics, we are finally allowed a glimpse into the ancient world of the Vedic Age.

---

[10]*Lost Languages* (2002) by Andrew Robinson, McGraw Hill, New York, page 331. (For the record, I am a so-called 'Dravidian' and not a North Indian who happens to agree with Jha and have authored a book with him.) Parpola's one useful contribution is the two-volume collection of photos of Indus seals. He has not read a single seal notwithstanding the pompous title of his book *Deciphering the Indus Script.* It is nothing but a jumble of anthropological speculation without a single useful insight into the Harappan language and script.

5.

Vedic people: Image of the ocean

Cultural biases

In this chapter I shall try to give a brief account of the nature of the society described in the *Rigveda.* It is a vast subject on which a great deal has been written—most of it conjectural and false—based more on preconceptions than on a careful study of the literature. My goal in this chapter is only to show that the *Rigveda* describes a society that was largely maritime. I will also indicate how this is finding support in archaeology not only of India, but also in finds as far away as Mexico and Peru. It should be noted that we are only beginning to find technical evidence of this kind, but we have at least made a beginning.

The dominant picture of the Vedic Aryans given in history books is that they were pastoral nomadic tribes of non-Indian origin. This is the picture presented in the works of nineteenth century (Christian) scholars like Max Müller, and their present day Indian followers of the Marxist school like Romila Thapar, R.S. Sharma and others. The latter school which has dominated the Indian history establishment since independence must be seen as the successor to the colonial-missionary school of Indian history and civilization, with Christian bias replaced by the Marxist.

To understand this formulation, it helps to look at the cultural milieu in which many European scholars labored, because it was Europeans who originated the idea; Indians have simply copied them without always understanding the underlying reasons and compulsions. In an interesting twist, American and European scholars are now beginning to give up on the invasion idea while many 'establishment' Indian scholars have tenaciously held on to it. American scholars, including authors of textbooks are increasingly following the model that resembles the one given here.

Nineteenth century scholars formulated their theories at a time when scientific data from archaeology and other fields did not exist. They were influenced by the Romantic Movement, which thought of evolution of societies in terms of pastoral tribes, upon which was superimposed their own cultural biases like Biblical beliefs, European colonial interests and the German nationalist movement. Later, when the discovery of Sanskrit showed Indian and European languages to be related, they interpreted Indian literature, notably the Vedas, in terms of their preconceptions while preserving their cultural biases. They claimed it to be the result of research in the new 'science' of comparative linguistics; but this was an afterthought—a rationalization of an idea that that had already taken root. It was a combination of cultural and social influences popular in nineteenth century Europe, with no basis in science.

Their modern Indian followers have kept the model—which may be called the colonial-missionary model—while giving it a Marxist twist. It should be noted that Marx was himself a product of nineteenth century Europe who had imbibed many of the same prejudices and cultural biases. Central to this new model is the idea of the Aryan invasion as a class conflict, entirely in keeping with the Marxist creed.

Beginning in this century, as we already saw, archaeological discoveries posed a serious challenge to this model. Archaeology, and perhaps even more significantly, data about ancient river systems and ecology shatter both the invasion model and the chronology of the Vedic Aryans found in history books. All this we already saw. A careful reading of the Vedic and Puranic literature, especially the *Rigveda* shows that the Vedic society has been grossly misrepresented by nineteenth century scholars and their present day followers.

Once we drop this preconception, a study of archaeology along with the *Rigveda* shows that from the earliest times the Vedic Aryans were a maritime people. Rivers and oceans played a very large part in their lives. This is reflected in the fact that oceanic symbolism is the most powerful of all found in the *Rigveda.* Thus they could hardly have been Central Asiatic nomads who never saw the ocean as Max Müller (and others) have claimed. His Indian followers today continue to repeat his claims without understanding the backgound and influence of the Romantic Movement under which he and most of his European colleagues grew up. As David Frawley has observed in the Foreword, their version of history is really a reflection of their cultural background and prejudices and has little to do with factual history.

Rigveda describes a maritime society

When we read the *Rigveda* in the original language, free from any preconceptions about nomadic people, what we find is a society dominated by maritime activity. References to oceans, ships and sailing are so numerous that one begins to wonder how anyone could have missed them. There are at least a hundred references to the sea in the *Rigveda.* The image of the ocean is the dominant poetic theme found in it. The Vedic poets describe the creation of the universe in terms of the ocean. Here is the famous creation hymn in David Frawley's fine translation. (The examples below are from the Rigvedic hymns X.129, X.72, X.149 and X190):

> In the beginning, there was darkness hidden in darkness,
> all this universe was an unillumined sea.
> The Gods stood together in the sea. Then as dancers
> they generated a swirl of dust.
> When, like ascetics, the Gods overflowed the world,
> then from hidden in the ocean they brought forth the Sun.
>
> The creative Sun upheld the Earth with lines of force.
> He strengthened the Heaven where there was no support.
> As a powerful horse he drew out the atmosphere.
> He bound fast the ocean in the boundless realm.
> Thence came the world and the upper region,
> thence Heaven and Earth were extended.
>
> Law and truth from the power of meditation were enkindled.
> Thence the night was born and then the flooding ocean.
> From the flooding ocean the year was born. The Lord of
> all that moves ordained the days and nights.
> The Creator formed the Sun and Moon according to previous
> worlds; Heaven and Earth, the atmosphere and the realm of light.

The whole of this passage is dominated by the image of the ocean. As Frawley has pointed out, a society totally ignorant of the sea does not visualize the creation myth itself in terms of the ocean.

It is said of the Eskimos, that because of their great familiarity with snow, they have many words for it in their language. Similarly, Vedic

Sanskrit also has numerous words for the sea often indicating finer nuances. Among the commonly used words are: *samudra, salila, sagara* and *sindhu.* The word *sindhu* can mean either the sea or a large river, and sometimes even the river Indus.

The etymology of the word *sindhu* is particularly interesting and sheds light on the Vedic society as a maritime society. It is derived from the root *sidh,* which means to go or to move. This is quite distinct from the root *sr* meaning to flow. From the root *sr* we get river names like Sarayu and Sarasvati, which were swift flowing rivers, at least in their upper reaches. Sindhu on the other hand was applied mainly to more navigable flows and the sea. It is interesting that one of the words for a mariner is *sindhuka* deriving also from the root *sidh.* And *sindhuka,* Sanskrit for sailor, became Sindbad the Sailor when stories from India found their way into the famous *Arabian Nights.*

Western India was then dominated by the delta of two great rivers—the Sarasvati and the Sindhu (Indus). These stretched from the west of the Rann of Kachch almost to Bhrigukaccha or the modern Broach. People of the Indus delta were known as Saindhavas, which can also mean maritime people deriving from the same root *sidh.* This vast coastal region into which flowed navigable rivers was ideal for the development of maritime civilization. Both the Vedic literature and satellite photographs indicate that the region was much better watered six thousand years ago than it is today. While the Sarasvati disappeared into the desert and ceased flowing from the 'mountain to the sea' probably before 3000 BC, the lower course of the Sarasvati emptied into the ocean in an enormous delta from the Rann to Prabhas and even beyond. The so-called Harappan Civilization was sustained largely by this flow. The Yadus, one of the most important of the Vedic people, and the clan to which Krishna himself belonged, were a western people from the present day Gujarat and Saurashtra regions.

All this indicates that Vedic society (of which Harappan was part, coming towards its end) was a complex mosaic in which riverine and ocean navigation played a major part. This helps explain the presence of many maritme and riverine stories in works like the *Mahabharata.* Bhisma is said to be the son of Ganga—a river goddess. This can mean that Ganga belonged to a river tribe that was part of a maritme society. The same is true of Satyavati whose father was the chief of a fishing tribe, from an area where there is now little fishing left. The word *apsara* (*ap-sara*), which is often taken to mean a celestial nymph or a mermaid, literally means 'she who moves in the waters'. Quite obviously this can refer to a woman from a maritime tribe.

So the many stories about *apsaras* found in ancient works simply indicate that women from maritime tribes often formed liaisons with men from more settled communities. Vedic seers like Vasistha and Agastya were said to be sons of apsaras, or women from maritme tribes. That their father was Varuna, the ocean, simply means that he belonged to an ocean going tribe. Just as Veda Vyasa was known as Dvaipayana or 'Son of the island' because he was born on an island. Vasistha was known as Maitra-Varuni or 'Son of Mitra of the ocean' meaning simply that he was a son of Mitra who was a member of a maritime tribe. Not surprisingly, references to the ocean, sea voyages and ships pervade the seventh book of the *Rigveda* whose authorship is attributed to the same Vasistha.

No ancient Indian work—beginning with the *Rigveda,* the Puranas, the epics—none of them, describes a nomadic people or society. They are the products of a settled civilization with a very large maritime component. If one wants to know what the epic of a nomadic people would be like, all one needs to do is study a Central Asiatic epic known as the *Secret History of the Mongols.* It was written to celebrate the exploits of the Mongol conqueror Chingis Khan and his people. It is nothing like any of the Indian works, let alone the Vedas.

Of all the statements made about the Vedic people and the Vedas, none is so baffling as the claim that the *Rigveda* does not know the ocean. Nothing could be further from the thruth. This should serve as a sobering pointer to the great deficiency of scholarship making such claims. When they have so grossly misinterpreted the Vedas by describing a maritime people as steppe nomads, what trust can we place in their worth?

Vedic people: Yadus and Purus

The two most important people of the *Rigveda* are the Purus (later known as Kurus) and the Yadus. As David Frawley has pointed out in his Foreword to the present book, the great Sarasvati River flowing from Kurukshetra of the Purus to the west coast where the Yadus lived would have connected these two ancient and important people. (Another branch of the Yadus lived in Mathura; the Yamuna served as a river link between the Kurus and the Yadus of the Mathura branch.) Since the great delta of the Sarasvati provided an outlet to the ocean, the maritime nature of the

Vedic society becomes easy to explain. This also explains how there was a concentration of Vedic seers in two places—the Bhrigus in the west, and the Vasisthas and Angirasas in the Kuru heartland. It is not in the least bit surprising that Vasistha of the seventh mandala shows great familiarity with maritime activity.

Since Vedic society, the Rigvedic society in particular, was mainly maritime with many more and much better watered rivers flowing in North India at the time, it may not be easy to locate and explore archaeological remains from that period. A maritime society like the one described in the *Rigveda* is not conducive to the preservation of artifacts in the usual sense. With the emergence of marine archaeology following the Second World War, there is now some hope that we may be able to find more about this ancient maritime culture. This is already happening, thanks to marine archaeology.

What is interesting is that some archaeological evidence is now beginning to surface, lending support to the idea that Vedic India had a strong maritime component. At an international conference on seafaring recently held in Delhi, several papers were presented showing that Indian cotton was exported to South- and Central America going back to 2500 BC and even earlier. One author presented evidence for the possible presence of Indian cotton in Mexico as far back as 4000 BC. According to Sean Mcgrail, a marine archaeologist at Oxford University, seagoing ships called 'clinkers' that were thought to be of Viking origin were known in India a good deal earlier. A PTI story filed on March 7, 1994 reported:

> Cotton from India reached Latin America at least 4000 years before Columbus, carried across the oceans by ancient mariners who had mastered long-distance navigation. That fascinating theory emerged at an international scientific meeting. Scholars from six countries also said that *ancient Indian boat-building and navigational skills have remained unrecognized.* (My emphasis.)
>
> "India was one of the earliest sites where maritime contacts flourished," said Jean-Francois Salles, a French archaeologist. "The bulk of the exchange between the 4500 year old Indus civilization and West Asia was by sea." The discovery that a hybrid variety of cotton was growing in America long before Columbus reached there in 1492 AD has triggered speculation that cotton from Asia, specifically India, was carried there well before 2500 BC.
>
> The northwest part of the Indian subcontinent had by 2500 BC established a very strong tradition of cotton. This makes India one of the most likely sites of origin of the cotton taken to the Americas. ...

> "Seafarers from this country [India] used constellations, the position of the pole star, and the movements of the sun to chart out nautical routes," said B. Arunachalam, ...
>
> The hybrid variety of cotton called 'tetraploid' cotton was growing in Mexico as early as 4000 years BC and fabrics based on this cotton dating back to 2500 BC have been found at a site called Husca Preita in Peru, ...

This means that Indian cotton could have reached Mexico before 4000 BC, taking us to the *Rigvedic Age.* We must recognize, however, that we have only begun to get technical evidence of this kind and we still have a long way to go. But we have enough already to show on the basis of the literary evidence of the *Rigveda,* that the Vedic society included a large maritime component. And this has begun to receive support from archaeology. It also explains why such a sophisticated harbor as Lothal was in operation by 2500 BC: it was needed to support this maritime trade. There would be no other reason for such extensive harbor works as found at Lothal and Dholavira.

What is important here is that all this is based on technical evidence and not some fanciful theories by linguists and anthropologists to support their preconceptions. Science is not the answer to everything, but it is certainly a better guide than prejudice.

Archaeology and literature: the Vedic Harappan connection

This brings us to what is undoubtedly the most important insight to emerge from the research of recent decades: *Harappan archaeology represents the material side of the civilization described in the Vedic literature.* Otherwise what we are left with is vast literature for the Vedic Aryans who left no archaeological traces, and mind-boggling archaeological remains of the Harappans who apparently left behind no literature. This is extraordinary to say the least, for both—Harappans and the Vedic Aryans flourished in the same geographical area. This is often called "Frawley's Paradox" because it was David Frawley who first highlighted this incongruity. And this is made doubly paradoxical when we note that the Harappans were literate, while the Vedic Aryans were supposed to be illiterate who depended on memorization. Yet it is the literature of the illiterate Aryans that has survived while the literate Harappans have vanished without a literary trace (see on page 68).

Jha's decipherment of the Indus script breaks this gridlock by showing that the Harappans were also Vedic people who used the Vedic language in

Vedic symbols in Harappan archaeology showing yogic postures (top), swasti signs and 'om' on a seal. The second line drawing shows how the *devanagari* om is derived from the Harappan om. Note the sacred *ashvattha* leaves on the om seal.

their seal inscriptions. This is described in the next chapter, but what I will do next is to show the Vedic identity of the Harappans without resort to the deciphered seals. The seals are replete with Vedic symbolism that is found also in the literature of the Veda and the Upanishads. Some of these including swastika symbols, the om sign and others are displayed in the plates. I find it remarkable that all this has been overlooked by scholars for nearly 80 years. The point is that the *Vedic-Harappan connection can be seen even without the help of the deciphered Indus seal inscriptions.* The position that Jha and this writer take is that the decipherment is a consequence of the Vedic-Harappan connection. Without recognizing the fact that the Harappan civilization was Vedic the writing cannot be read.

To see this Vedic-Harappan connection, one can begin with the practice of Yoga, which is Vedic in origin. There is strong evidence that the Harappans practiced yoga. The figure displays several terra cotta figurines in yogic postures or *asanas.* These were found at various sites like Harappa and Mohenjo-Daro.

To see this connection further, one can focus on familiar sacred symbols like the swastika signs. Harappan sites are replete with the swastika. Swastika stands for *svasti-ka,* meaning 'maker of welfare'. They appear singly as well as in combination with other signs. The photo shows a string of five swastikas. This is related to the sacred *panca-svasti mantra* found in the *Yajurveda* (25.18–19), in which the word 'svasti' (welfare) appears five times. It may be paraphrased as:

We invoke Him who may bring us welfare.
May the respected Indra guard our welfare,
May the omniscient Pushan guard our welfare,
May the Universal Creator guard our welfare,
May the Great Protector bring us welfare.

These invocations appear also in the *Rigveda.* The Harappan swastika string is obviously related to this Vedic prayer. Such connections are not limited to the *Rigveda* and the *Yajurveda*; they span the whole gamut of the Vedic literature, including the *Brahmanas, Upanishads* and others.

Another important Vedic symbol appearing on Harappan artifacts is the OM sign, known also as *pranavakshara.* The plate shows the seal known as 'Onkara Mudra' or the Om seal. The same figure displays also line drawings of the seal in two positions—original and rotated by 90 degrees. The one on the right—i.e. rotated by 90 degrees—is obviously the source of the Devanagari 'om'. Southern scripts like Kannada and Telugu have retained the original orientation of the Harappan 'Om', while elongating it a little. All of them derive from the Harappan 'Om' and have deep connections with Vedic thought as follows. The photo and the line drawings display only the most ornate Om signs found; the same signs appear on scores of Harappan artifacts in unadorned style.

This 'bow-shaped' Harappan 'Om' carries profound Vedic symbolism. It is described at many places in the Vedic literature. The *Mundaka Upanishad* (2.2.4) describes it as: "Pranava (Om) is the bow, the soul is the arrow, Brahma is the target. With full concentration, aim at the target and strike, to become one with Brahma, just as the arrow becomes one with the target." This is almost a visual description of 'Om' as found on the Harappan seal displayed.

The 'Om', which is adorned by *ashvattha* leaves and branches, highlights the sacredness attributed to the *ashvattha,* a Vedic idea. The *Katha Upanishad* (2.3.1) describes the *ashvattha* (pipul) tree as embodying the essence of sacredness: "This is the eternal *ashvattha* tree, with the root at the top (*urdhvamoolo*), but branches downwards. It is He that is called the Shining One and Immortal. All the worlds are established in Him, none transcends Him." The same idea is echoed in the *Bhagavadgita* (15.1): "He who knows that *ashvattha* tree with its root above and branches down, whose leaves are the Vedas said to be imperishable. And he who knows it knows the Vedas."

In all this there is the symbolism of the *ashvattha* as the seat of sacred knowledge (or Veda), and the abode of the Gods. This idea goes back to the *Rigveda* itself (X.97.5): "Your abode is the *ashvattha* tree, your dwelling is made of its leaves." With such explicit Vedic symbolism, there cannot be the slightest doubt that Harappan archaeology contains physical representations of Vedic ideas. What is given here is a miniscule sample of the Vedic symbolism that pervades Harappan archaeology. It is discussed in more detail in the book *The Deciphered Indus Script* by N. Jha and this writer.

In summary, the Vedic and Harappan civilizations were one. Harappan artifacts are material representations of ideas and thoughts found in the Vedic literature. The Harappans therefore were Vedic Harappans.

6.

Language puzzle: Vedic India and Europe

Background: origin and spread of ancient peoples

The implications for ancient history of this scientifically derived chronological framework are far-reaching. We shall soon see that it has also the potential to unlock the secret of Indo-European languages: to wit, why people from India and Sri Lanka to England and Iceland speak languages clearly related to one another.

It has been known for at least two centuries that Indian and European languages are related. What is *deva* in Sanskrit is *deus* in Latin, *theo* in Greek and *dieu* in French. What is *agni* (fire) in Sanskrit becomes *ignis* in Latin from which we get modern English words like ignite and ignition. These affinities go deeper. This recognition was partly what was responsible for the creation of the Aryan invasion theory. But as we saw before, linguists combined it with racial ideas current in 19th century Europe and modified them to suit their own requirements. This is what gave rise to the modern discipline called Indo-European studies though its followers strenuously deny its racist origins.

This was simply an easy way out of a challenging problem: take an existing idea and fit new data to it and pretend we have a new 'linguistic' theory with language replacing race. We also saw that science has demolished this theory. This means they failed to build a new scientific model as demanded by the new data. So what we need is an alternative explanation to account for the close similarities we find between Indian and European languages. Fortunately such an alternative reconstruction is now taking place thanks to the work of several scholars, notably Shrikant Talageri. But it calls for a radical change in our perception of history of civilizations.

Historians have always told us that civilization began in the river valleys of Mesopotamia in the early third millennium BC. This is several thousand years too late; we now know that most of the *Rigveda* had been *completed* nearly a thousand years earlier. The beginning of the Rigvedic Age and of ancient India must now be placed well before that. Vedic scholars like David Frawley and Lokamanya Tilak have found references in the *Rigveda* pointing to dates before 6000 BC. Personally speaking I prefer to be more conservative, but I have no difficulty placing important episodes as far back as 4600 BC. (This is a conservative dating assuming c. 3700 BC for the end of the Rigvedic Age and the Battle of Ten Kings.)

In fact, at around that date of c. 4600 BC (conservative), an Indian ruler known as Mandhata conducted a series of campaigns in the northwest of India against a people recorded in ancient works as the Druhyus. The Druhyus suffered a massive defeat.

This forced them to leave India and there was a large-scale emigration into Central Asia and possibly as far west as Europe. In addition to linguistic affinities, similarities in myths and beliefs show that ancient Indians and Europeans must at one time have been in close contact. Otherwise it is difficult to explain why for instance a language like Lithuanian is so close to Sanskrit, or, why Teutonic, Celtic and Hindu mythologies show such strong affinities. Although we cannot yet fully answer the question, we are beginning to make progress thanks to the brilliant work of the young linguist and historian Shrikant Talageri.

Vedic history: Mandhata's campaign

Based on a detailed linguistic and cultural analysis, Talageri has suggested that many of the ancient European practices could have evolved from this immigrant wave following Mandhata's campaign against the Druhyus. This does not necessarily mean that Europe was populated by these immigrants, but only that pagan Europe received and incorporated many of its ideas and languages from these immigrants, just as China, Japan and the Far East received Buddhism and Buddhist mythologies from India many centuries later. Their existing languages were also influenced and modified just as English was by the infusion of French following the Norman Conquest of England in 1066 AD. Among the people driven out by Mandhata's campaign in Northwest India were the Druhyus who are recorded in the *Rigveda* as a very ancient people.

These Druhyus, according to Talageri, came to be known as the Druids (Celtic priests) in ancient Europe. The Druids themselves traced their origins to Asia, and dated their arrival in Europe to just before 3900 BC. The word Druid may be derived from the Sanskrit 'dru-vid' meaning 'forest knowledge'. It is cognate with a class of ancient Indian texts called *Aranyakas* or 'forest books' because they were conceived and taught by sages living in forest hermitages. It must be kept in mind that this is just informed guesswork. It still needs a good deal more evidence.

While this is in broad agreement with the c. 4600 BC date for Mandhata's campaign, it is important to note that there is as yet has no archaeological or other hard scientific support. It is yet a tantalizing possibility. But few scholars have bothered to look at ancient European archaeology with this possibility in mind. Ancient European history and culture have been heavily colored by Christian biases. It was only in the period following the Renaissance that Europeans began to look back to their heritage of Greece with pride and admiration bordering on awe. Now almost all Europeans look back to the pagan civilization of Greece as their Golden Age rather than to Medieval Europe dominated by Christianity; the latter they call the Dark Ages. But their notion of Greece and the Greek civilization still carries biases acquired through two thousand years of association with Christianity. They cannot see Greece as the Greeks saw themselves.

(The Greek Civilization was quite similar to the Hindu. Socrates, Aristotle and Plato would have fitted in very well with the sages of the Upanisads, except no one would have demanded that Socrates be killed.)

During the Middle Age, often called the Dark Age, the Church, which dominated all aspects of life in Europe tried to obliterate every trace of earlier civilizations. (They did the same in the Americas after the voyages of discovery where several ancient civilizations were destroyed.) In a massive effort the Europeans succeeded in recapturing a part of the lost glory of their pagan past from what was left of the heritage of Greece.

A similarly enlightened attitude, if carried over into the study of all of ancient Europe, may begin to yield a great deal more about our ancient past. For instance, a huge silver cup bearing the stamp of 'Pashupati' dating to c. 150 BC has been found in Denmark: it is known as the 'Gundenstrup Cauldron'. The image on it is very similar to that of the Pashupati found on Harappan seals created two thousand years earlier. This also indicates a westward movement of Indian influence. It is merely a foretaste of what still remains to be discovered, once we drop our preconceptions about the Aryan invasion.

The Battle of Ten Kings

Returning to Vedic India, then as now the northwest of India was a turbulent region. Nearly a thousand years after Mandhata's campaign against the Druhyus, Vedic king Sudas had to deal with a confederation led by the Druhyus and other people from the west and the northwest. The result was the famous Battle of Ten Kings recorded by Vasishta in the seventh book of the *Rigveda;* it is one of the major historical episodes to be found in the *Rigveda*. This battle may be placed around 3750 BC. This dating is on the conservative side as I noted earlier.

Sudas is an important historical figure. He was the patron of the famous Vedic seers Vasishta and Vishwamitra. The compilation of the *Rigveda* into its various books seems to have begun in his time. It was completed more than five centuries later by Vasishta's descendant Krishna-Dvaipayana who is better known as Veda Vyasa, which means 'organizer of the Vedas.' He is famous also as the author of the great *Mahabharata.*

To return to the Battle of Ten Kings—the *Rigveda* calls it *dasharajna*—was one of the pivotal episodes of ancient history. Among the people defeated and driven out by Sudas were the Prithu-Parthavas, the Parsus, the Alinas and several others mentioned in the *Rigveda*. The Prithu-Parthavas of course are known as the Parthians whose descendants founded a great empire in Iran; the Parthians in fact called themselves Parthava. The Parsus became the Persians and the Alinas are the Hellenes or the ancient Greeks, according to some scholars.

Other opponents of Sudas included Pakthas and Balhanas. Their descendants are known today as Pathans (or Pakthoons) and Baluchis of the Bolan Pass. Talageri notes several others. Thus, many of the so-called Indo-European peoples of the ancient world can be traced to India in very ancient times. This incidentally also helps explain why people from India to Iceland speak languages similar to one another and have also related mythologies. They probably were the original Indo-European carriers of myths and languages, which became over laden upon the people already living in Europe.

(For the record I reject the idea of a single root language like Proto Indo-European. I hold that if this scenario is correct, Sanskrit might have influenced existing languages in Europe, just as French influenced English after the Norman Conquest. Sanskrit similarly influenced Indian and Southeast Asian languages.)

Vedic India and pre-historic Europe

There is now tantalizing archaeological evidence from Europe pointing to a similar conclusion: it suggests the presence of an earlier layer of civilization there also before the rise of the material civilizations of Egypt, Mesopotamia and the Indus Valley. This is the result of revisions taking place in European prehistory, arising from what the British archaeologist Colin Renfrew calls the 'second radiocarbon revolution'. According to Renfrew, we now have a revolution in the making in our understanding of prehistoric Europe and its relationship to the ancient Near East. He tells us:

> Most of us have been brought up to believe, for instance, that the Pyramids of Egypt are the oldest stone-built monuments in the world, and that the first temples built by man were situated in the Near East, in the fertile land of Mesopotamia. ... (Renfrew 1990: p 16)
>
> It comes, then, as a shock to learn that all this is wrong. The megalithic chamber tombs of Western Europe are now dated earlier than the Pyramids ... The traditional view of prehistory is now contradicted at every point. (*ibid*)

This radical transformation is the result of revised of radiocarbon dates brought about by recalibration with the help of tree rings. It is unnecessary to go into technical details of 'dendrochronology'; it is enough to know that the radiocarbon method tends greatly to underestimate ancient dates— by as much as *800 years* when applied to dates like 3000 BC; there are examples in Renfrew's book that show dates moving from 3000 BC to almost 4000 BC. (This suggests that many of the dates assigned to sites and artifacts in India are probably underestimates.) To continue with Renfrew:

> Already, twenty years ago, the new scientific technique of radiocarbon dating brought archaeologists several surprises. But it did not challenge the basic assumption underlying what they had written: the position of the ancient civilizations of Egypt and Mesopotamia as the innovators, illuminating the rest of the Old World with the radiance of their culture was not changed. Today the second radiocarbon revolution, based on recent advances in tree-ring dating, has undermined these assumptions. (Renfrew 1990: pp. 16-17)

This means that the whole concept Mesopotamia as the cradle of civilization is under assault, with revised dates striking "what seems a decisive blow at the whole framework of thought which has dominated archaeological discussion until very recent times." (*ibid*) To place things in perspective, the second radiocarbon revolution tells us that a *prehistoric civilization of Europe was in place before the rise of Mesopotamia and Egypt.* That is to say, the reversal of the time relationship between the Vedic Aryans and the Harappans (and the Sumerians) that we see in ancient India has its counterpart in prehistoric Europe. But unlike India with its abundant Vedic and Puranic literary records, Europe has no literary records to speak of beyond faint memories in its myth and folklore. The spread of Christianity obliterated all traces of Europe's prehistoric past. Turning again to Renfrew:

> The new dating helps us to see that we have been underestimating those creative 'barbarians' of prehistoric Europe. It now seems that they were erecting monuments in stone, smelting copper, setting up solar observatories [like the Stonehenge] and doing other ingenious things without any help from east Mediterranean. (*ibid*)

This reversal in perspective is due entirely to advances in dating techniques. The 'creative barbarians' of Europe may have received some of their language and other cultural traits from the pre-Harappan Vedic India—as Talageri suggests. It is time perhaps to re-examine the archaeological finds in Europe in the light of this possible connection. The Gundestrup Cauldron (Thompson 1992) with its impression of the famous 'Pashupati' found also on Harappan seals is a pointer to other connections that remain to be found.

As Renfrew puts the question: "... if barbarian [i.e., pre-Christian] Europe did not acquire its important innovations from the Near East, how did they come about?"

The arguments and the evidence given in this book suggest that it came at least in part from Vedic India. This was perhaps true more of language and religious thought than technology itself. Talageri had arrived at this conclusion without the benefit of the changes in the interpretation of European archaeology noted by Renfrew. I was also not aware of these radical changes in the European perspective when I arrived at similar conclusions relating to Vedic India and the Near East based on literary and scientific records. All three point to the existence of this civilization in India as well as in Europe before the dawn of civilizations in the Near East. It was probably a world civilization with a significant maritime component.

This, I suggest, was the primeval world of the Vedic Aryans—a mainly spiritual world before the rise of the material civilizations of Egypt, Mesopotamia and the Indus. *krnvanto visvamarya*—'let us make the whole world Aryan'—says the *Rigveda.* It acquires fresh meaning in view of the new light being shed on Vedic India and prehistoric Europe. It is time that we combine the finds of Vedic India with those of prehistoric Europe and see what the world before the dawn was really like. It was a mainly spiritual world. It would be seriously wrong to interpret it entirely in material terms as archaeologists are prone to do. The Vedas are there to give us insight into their thinking and even language.

European languages

As far as European languages are concerned, what resulted was in all probability a blending with existing languages—like what happened to English following the Norman Conquest in 1066 AD. They were Indo-European only in the sense that Indian myths, practices and languages became part of the mix. The same thing happened to Indian languages like Hindi, Urdu and Marathi; Persian words and usages became mixed with the Indian. It is a myth of modern linguistics to think that all Indian and European languages can be traced to a single source language called Proto Indo-European. This is contradicted by empirical evidence, especially when quantitative tests are applied. (More on this later.)

Field studies with American Indian languages show that more primitive a region, the greater the variability in languages. Language barriers come down due to advances in technology like printing, and now television. So, if anything, there were *more, not fewer* languages in ancient times. A language like Sanskrit must have evolved as a synthesis of different languages to be used as a common medium. The very name—'Samskrita' meaning 'cultivated'—suggests such a possibility. It became a very rich language by being used by different people speaking different languages, just as English has become very rich because it is used as the common medium by a large number of people many of whom speak other languages. So the idea of a common ancestor for a family of languages is contradicted by real world experience. And the same linguists claim that somehow the Harappans managed to retain their linguistic identity with a separate Dravidian family, moving a thousand miles to the south, while everyone else—from East India to Iceland became Indo-European speakers!

It should also be noted that the languages and cultures of Southeast Asian countries like Indonesia, Cambodia, Thailand and others also show the influence of Sanskrit and Hindu culture. This is because they were heavily influenced by Indians who moved into these countries. This happened in historical times as with the Shailendra Empire and the Cholas. Both were maritime kingdoms—exactly like the Vedic Aryans. But if we apply the Aryan invasion idea to explain this, we would have to invent a Southeast Asian invasion of India.

The scenario given here—of migrations out of India rather than an Aryan invasion—upsets not only the Aryan invasion theory, but the whole version of ancient history. The Indian Aryans were not a branch of the Indo-Europeans, but were in fact the source from which the people who may be called Indo-Europeans drew some of their linguistic and cultural fruits. Further, far from there being any Aryan invasion, there were repeated emigrations from India stemming from a combination of ecological and political disturbances in the Vedic heartland. This is precisely what one should expect when there are large-scale disturbances in a densely populated region. Noting the presence of Indian names and gods among the Mittani of Syria and the Hittites of Asiatic Turkey in the 15th century BC, F.E. Pargiter observed long ago:

> These facts prove (1) that there was an outflow of people from India before the fifteenth century BC; (2) that they brought Aryan gods from India; (3) that therefore Aryans and their gods existed in India before the sixteenth century; and (4) that the Aryans had entered India earlier still. These facts and conclusions are hardly reconcilable with the current theory about the entrance of the Aryans into NW [northwest] India ...
>
> But these facts and conclusions are in full agreement with what tradition says about the outspread of the Druhyus beyond the north-west of India ...(Pargiter 1922: pp 301-302)

Pargiter's analysis has never been refuted even though his absolute chronology can no longer be supported. But he was writing at a time when he had no data from archaeology or other scientific sources. He went on further to point out that all the sacred spots of the Hindus are in the east, in the middle Himalayas; there are no Hindu places of pilgrimage in Afghanistan, Iran or other lands to the north and west. Although his chronology and many of the conclusions derived from them have been overtaken by the research results of the past 70 years, his literary analysis of the Puranas remains valuable. His absolute dates based on 950 BC for the Mahabharata War cannot be sustained in the face of all the scientific discoveries since he wrote his book; his compilation of dynastic lists leading to his relative chronology however remains a fundamental contribution though it is not without error.

Talageri takes it further. While Pargiter concentrated on an analysis of the Puranic dynastic lists, Talageri analyzed both the languages and ancient Indian and European myths. Let us hear what Talageri has to say about the migrations recorded in the Puranas:

> And then the Puranas make the most amazing and clear declaration of the emigration of major sections of these Druhyus from Afghanistan to strange and distant land in the north. The evidence provided by this unique statement is so absolute that no honest scholar can deny that it constitutes evidence of the migration of Indo-Europeans. (Talageri 1993: pp 327-8)
>
> Among the speakers of Indo-European languages, a great historical occurrence took place when a major part of the Indo-Europeans of the south-eastern Uttar Pradesh migrated to the west and settled down in the northwestern areas—Punjab, Kashmir and the further northwest where they differentiated into three groups: the Purus (in the Punjab), the Anus (in Kashmir) and the Druhyus (in the northwest and Afghanistan).
>
> The Purus [and later the Kurus] developed the Vedic culture of the Punjab, ...
>
> Meanwhile, major sections of Anus spread out over Western Asia and developed into the various Iranian cultures. The Druhyus spread out into Europe in two installments: the speakers of the proto-Germanic dialect first migrated northwards and then westwards, and then later the speakers of the proto-Hellenic and proto-Italic-Celtic dialects moved into Europe by a different, more southern route. (Talageri 1993: 367)

As can be seen, this is a bold hypothesis that is at the same time well supported by linguistics and also by the connections found between the mythologies of the various ancient peoples. Talageri holds that the Aryan dynasties originated in the east and then spread westwards, which was also the view of Pargiter. Talageri's model should be validated through archaeological and other scientific data.

New light from quantitative tests

All these theories about Indo-Europeans and their origins depend heavily on the similarity of sounds and structure found among Indian and European languages. To one familiar with the exact sciences, the basis for these theories seems extraordinarily vague. While there are many technical sounding terms and verbal arguments, there are almost no attempts at applying quantitative methods. When outsiders (read non-linguists), apply such methods the results don't support many of the claims of these theories.

When mathematicians Kruskal, Dyen and Black applied statistical tests to the languages that make up the Indo-European family the results were extraordinary. (Kruskal, Dyen, Black, 1971.) The most important member of the Indo-European family is Sanskrit, but their analysis threw up a major contradiction: Indian and Iranian languages failed the grouping test! This is a bombshell, for according to Indo-European linguistics, Indo-Iranian is the lynchpin of the whole discipline, but the one quantitative test that was applied to the hypothesis discredited it.

No less a scientist than Cavalli-Sforza was stunned by the negative result. He noted with surprise, that the Kruskal, Dyen and Black study "...found no similarity at all between Italic and Celtic languages, nor between Indian and Iranian ones... The non-identification of an Indo-Iranian group by Dyen, et al. is the major departure from the conclusions accepted by the majority of traditional linguists." (*Great Human Diasporas,* Addison-Wesley, 1995: page 190.) Recently, Cavalli-Sforza and his colleagues also note that genetic data don't support the linguistic, or caste and/or race based division of the Indian population.[1]

It is the same story with another invasion/migration theory known as the Kurgan homeland theory of Indo European speakers. (This refers to prehistoric settlements in the region north of the Black Sea in Ukraine.) Since there are no genetic methods for detecting what language a people spoke thousands of years ago—or speak today—its proponents have to exercise considerable ingenuity in support of their theory. This they have done. The Kurgan people have left no written records of any kind. Noting this Cavalli-Sforza observes: "Without written documents, it is very difficult for archaeologists to say what language was spoken in this region at the time." Difficult? Impossible seems a better description.

Apparently, the argument for the Kurgan inhabitants as the original Indo European speakers is based on the fact that some horses have been

[1]Kisivild, et. al., op.cit. The Kruskal, Dyen, Black study is so devastating to Indo-European linguistics that linguists dare not even mention it, pretending that it doesn't exist. This neagationist tactic is now being applied to genetic tests, which too contradict their theories.

found buried in the region. (The logic of this escapes this writer who happens to be a mathematical scientist.) This horse argument appears to be a favorite with the Aryan invasion theorists though it has repeatedly been discredited.

It is important to interpret these negative results properly. For example the failure of the statistical tests to show any relationship between Indian and Iranian languages does not mean that they are unrelated. *It means that the methodology and the conclusions on which the Indo-Iranian theory is built lacks scientific support.* The same applies to other negative results stemming from the statistical tests.

To return to Talageri's work, while I admire the brilliance of his research and the boldness of his conception, I am not entirely comfortable with his reliance on hypothetical languages like proto-Germanic and proto-Hellenic. It is not necessary, however, to agree with him in every detail to recognize that he has made a major contribution to the ancient puzzle of Indo-European languages. The general idea that the languages and the culture spread westwards from India now appears beyond doubt. As I observed in the previous section, we now have archaeological evidence from Europe attesting to the existence of a European civilization predating Egypt and Mesopotamia.

All this dovetails nicely with Talgeri's conclusions. This has the merit of agreeing with the views about prehistoric Europe described by Colin Renfrew as a result of the 'Second Radiocarbon Revolution'. Since the Vedic civilization was flourishing in India well before 4000 BC, only such a westward expansion appears possible.

More on genetics and ancient populations

Talageri's main conclusion based on his study of ancient languages and literature is that human movements in ancient times was mainly from east to west rather than west (and northwest) to east and south into the Indian subcontinent as claimed by colonial scholars and their modern followers. (It is best to ignore the likes of Asko Parpola who have done little more than dress up political slogans in academic language.) What is interesting is that we now have evidence from prehistoric human DNA samples that tell us the same thing. First, genetic data, both mitochondrial DNA (female line) and Y-chromosomes (male lineage), are clear that the Indian population has evolved locally going back tens of thousands of years, and not changed much due to any recent migrations. (By 'recent' we mean a few centuries or even millennia.) Here is Cavalli-Sforza's conclusion cited in the previous chapter, reproduced for convenient reference.

> Taken together, these results show that Indian tribal and caste populations derive largely from the same genetic heritage of Pleistocene southern and western Asians *and have received limited gene flow from external regions since the Holocene.* The phylogeography [neighboring branches] of the primal mtDNA and Y-chromosome founders suggests that these southern Asian Pleistocene coastal settlers from Africa would have provided the inocula for the subsequent differentiation of the distinctive eastern and western Eurasian gene pools. (Italics added.)

This means that the earliest Indian population centers were coastal settlements from where they expanded into the interior. Recent studies, notably by Stephen Oppenheimer advance it further in two respects. In his *Out of Eden*[2] Oppenheimer gives also an approximate date: modern humans have lived in South Asia, i.e., in an area south of the line from Yemen to Eastern Himalayas, for *at least* 70,000 years. No less significantly, he further observes that *all non-African humans living in the world today are descendants of these ancient South Asian people.*

This means, all modern humans of the world—Europeans, Chinese, Southeast Asians, American Indians, Australian aborigines, and so forth—each and every group of them is descended from South Asians who were the first people to leave Africa and survive outside Africa. It is worth noting that scientists believe that modern humans evolved in Africa and then spread to the rest of the world. What scientists are now saying is that the oldest population group (outside Africa) happens to be South Asian, for at least the last 70,000 years. Further, Indians have received hardly any gene flow from outside in the past ten thousand years (since the Holocene or since the last Ice Age ended).

This also makes ecological sense. During the early Holocene period, tropical Asia, especially the Indian seacoast, was one of the few areas that supported large human populations. As described in the next section, North India became habitable only because the ending of the Ice Age released the Himalayan rivers making the northern plains fertile. Before that it was arid and unsuitable for the kind of society described in the *Rigveda.*

---

[2]Published by Constable, London (2003).

What about Europeans? When and from where did they come? Here the genetic evidence is quite clear. Unlike South Asians, Europeans did not migrate directly from Africa but from South Asia. That is to say, they are twice removed from our African ancestors. A branch of South Asians possibly from Yemen all the way east to India (or via the Middle East) migrated and settled in Europe. When did this happen? About 40,000 to 50,000 years ago according to current estimates, possibly later. Genetic data indicates a second movement from North India through Kashmir and Central Asia via a more northerly route somewhat later.

That is to say, far from any invasion (or migration) from Europe (or Eurasia) into India, there were migrations in the opposite direction. But the time scale is vastly different—not thousands of years but tens of thousands. Even this is subject to upward revision. A point to note is that historians and linguists have very greatly underestimated the time scales, by as much as a factor of ten.

Where does all this leave linguistic theories—about Indo-European, proto-Indo-European and so forth, not to speak of proto-Dravidian and other hypothetical languages? Nowhere. Not only have the linguists got the direction of movements wrong, they have also used time scales that are miniscule. There is something else interesting. Note that the earliest human settlements in India were in the coastal regions—that is to say South India. *This means the oldest Indian languages must also have existed in the south.*

Does this mean that the Rigvedic language and its descendants like Vedic Sanskrit and others originated in the South? This is a distinct possibility, certainly a major field for research. It helps account for the profuse oceanic symbolism found in the *Rigveda.* But we should be willing to consider much longer time horizons and also free ourselves from nineteenth century race- and linguistic theories. They now lie in shambles like the Aryan invasion.

It is not hard to see that this calls for a major reorientation in our thinking. Simple-minded invasion theories and linguistic models just won't work. What we need now are scientifically rigorous multidisciplinary approaches.

From the Ice Age to the Great Drought

The next question: why was there such an extraordinary literary and intellectual flowering as seen in the Vedas and the Sutras in ancient India, and what happened to it? The answer to the question is to be found probably in the unique ecology of the region following the last Ice Age. The Ice Age began to end, in fits and starts, some 10,000 years ago.[3] This meant an abundant supply of water into the plains of India derived from the melting of accumulated ice caps to the north. Even today, the great rivers of North India are fed by the Himalayan glaciers. For several thousand years, water from the melting ice caps turned most of North India into a vast parkland—a veritable Garden of Eden. Many areas like Sind, Rajasthan and Baluchistan that are now arid were then fertile and supported large populations.

This is now confirmed both by archaeology and satellite photography. Satellite photographs have shown that numerous natural flows once existed in areas that are now dry. In Cholistan—in the Bahawalpur district of Pakistan—archaeologists have found hundreds of Harappan and pre Harappan sites. Some of them date back to 3500 BC and earlier; when proper corrections are applied, some of them will probably go back to 4000 BC. The Cholistan area is now arid and sparsely populated.

But this age of water abundance could not last forever. In the course of several millennia, the stock of ice began to be depleted, putting increasing pressure on the land that by then was probably overpopulated. These factors forced people living at the periphery to descend on the Sarasvati heartland in search of water and more productive land. The emigrations following Mandhata's campaign against the Druhyus as well as the Battle of Ten Kings should be attributed as much to ecological pressures as to the military campaigns of Mandhatr and Sudas. According to this scenario, the dispersal of Indo-Europeans from the Indus-to-Ganges heartland resulted from a combination of ecological and political upheavals.

I want to emphasize that what is presented here is NOT another invasion scenario—or an Aryan invasion theory of Europe! We may see it simply as a migration of people who carried with them the seeds of Indo-Aryan culture—language, religion and mythology—that was later planted in far off lands. These were people from a densely populated heartland seeking their fortunes in less populated areas—more like the Pilgrim Fathers than the Spanish Conquistadors.

---

[3]As noted previously, this is an oversimplification that ignores the freezing spells known the Older and the Younger Dryas. The Holocene or the post-Ice Age period is more complex than previously thought.

Our best guess at this time is that these waves of migration were due to a combination of ecology and politics. We see the Hindus doing this even today—carrying their culture into Europe and America, building temples and preserving ancient practices in howsoever a diluted form. The Swaminarain Temple in London built in 1995 is already being hailed as one of the architectural masterpieces of Europe and attracting many devotees and tourists. There are hundreds of Hindu temples being built in Europe and North America.

The picture then can be reconstructed as follows. During the Rigvedic Age, that is before 3700 BC, the greatest and the holiest of the rivers was the Sarasvati, which flowed through the present day Rajasthan and parts of Sind. North India was then a continuous tract of fertile land with no intervening Thar Desert to divide the Punjab from the Gangetic plane. Gradually this river also began to grow weaker. Already by the time of the Mahabharata War (c. 3100 BC) the river disappeared into the desert. One result of this was the division of the country and of the Vedic culture into the Eastern and the Western peoples.

This split is reflected in the Vedic literature also. The Eastern school which was concentrated first around the Kuru-Pancala country (Delhi, Haryana, and West UP) moving eventually to Magadha, became the home of religious orthodoxy and a fertile school for philosophic speculation and world religions. Moving west and southwest was the Taittiriya branch of Vedic learning, which excelled in the natural sciences—especially mathematics. Baudhayana, one of the world's first great mathematicians whose work is still preserved, came from the Taittiriya school. The great grammarian Panini, a supreme rationalist was also a Westerner. It is therefore no accident that the great urban civilization of the Harappans sprang in this area beginning shortly before 3000 BC. It is also no accident that most of the religious reform movements like Buddhism and Jainism should have originated in the east, in Magadha.

This sheds interesting light on our own civilization, its popular (and over-simple) division into Eastern mysticism and Western rational sciences and technology. The roots of both may be sought in the East-West split of the world's Vedic heritage going back perhaps to 3000 BC. The seed of the material civilization was the Harappan world, which sprang from the rational sciences of the Vedic Age. The *Sulbasutras* are prime examples of such creations. This is now supported by scientific findings.

Seidenberg has shown that all of ancient mathematics—Egyptian, Babylonian and the Greek—is derived from the *Sulbasutras.* For this reason he called the Sulbas the 'Origin of mathematics'. Harappans also excelled in metallurgy. Until the beginning of the Industrial Revolution, India produced the world's finest steels. Jha has suggested that alphabetic writing was also invented by the Harappans—as seen on the famous Harappan seals. (This is discussed in a later chapter.) Thus two of the greatest inventions of mankind—mathematics and alphabetical writing—have Vedic roots. One may dispute it, but it is certainly an important topic for research.

Eastern philosophy and religions—Upanishads, Buddhism, Jainism and even Zoroastrianism—all have roots in the same primordial source. The Western world has never been the source of any religion, though theocracy—which is the pursuit economic and political goals in the name of religion—appears to have been a Western, or at least a Middle Eastern innovation. West has now all but rejected a spiritual approach to human problems; in the name of 'secular humanist,' it is now strictly a materialistic civilization. At the same time, it has rejected also theocracy. It was the rejection of Church theocracy that made the West secular-humanistic.

In summary: the Harappans were not only part of the Vedic Aryan society, but in fact the Vedic Age ended with them. The seeds of both Eastern philosophy and Western rationalism can be found in the Vedic tradition. The Vedas, and more particularly the *Rigveda* belong to an earlier layer of civilization before the rise of Egypt, Sumeria and the Indus Valley. This was the world of the primeval Aryans—a culture, not a race—the soil from which grew the mighty Indo-European tree. This appears to be the verdict of science.

7.

Vedic age: On the banks of the Sarasvati

A world before the dawn

What science now tells us about ancient India and the world is appears to be at odds with what history books have to say about the dawn of civilization. The cradle of civilization was not the Mesopotamia of the Tigris-Euphrates rivers. The Sumerian civilization of Mesopotamia was contemporary with the Harappan; if anything, the Harappan was slightly earlier. This belongs to the Sutra period that came at the end of the Vedic Age; the age that preceded it—the age of the Brahmanas and the four Vedas—belongs to an earlier layer of civilization before the rise of Egypt, Mesoptamia and the Indus Valley (Harappan). The Harappan (Sutra) period was the twilight of this great primeval civilization whose antecedents go back to the ending of the last Ice Age itself. The *Rigveda* is a living remnant of this primeval age. A young French scholar, Jean Le Meé, observed (1975, p ix):

> Precious stones or durable materials—gold, silver, bronze, marble, onyx or granite—have been used by most ancient people in an attempt to immortalize their achievements. Not so however the Aryans. They turned what may seem the most volatile and insubstantial material of all—the spoken word—and out of this bubble of air fashioned a monument which for more than thirty, perhaps forty centuries later stands untouched by time or the elements.

How much greater the wonder of Le Meé should be when he learns that the *Rigveda* has withstood the ravages of time not for thirty or forty centuries, but as we now know, for at least sixty or even eighty centuries? A wonder indeed! To continue with Le Meé:

> ... the pyramids have been eroded by the desert wind, the marble broken by earthquakes, and the gold stolen by robbers, while the Veda is recited daily by an unbroken chain of generations, traveling like a great wave through the living substance of mind.

Thanks to this matchless feat of preservation, the Vedas are in a better state of preservation than many a stone inscription. The Vedas are preeminently the records of a culture of which spirituality was the major component; their spiritual vision made them see themselves as part of nature. They most certainly are not a record of the history of a nomadic people. It was a blunder of the first magnitude to try and write ancient history by treating the Vedas as relatively recent imports. In addition to the unscientific foundation of nineteenth century European scholarship, the idea that the Vedas, especially the *Rigveda,* contain the early history of the invading Aryans has been a great barrier to an objective study of ancient India. A good part of the history of Vedic India is to be found in the Puranas, a word that means ancient chronicles. The late F.E. Pargiter, undoubtedly the foremost Western student of the Puranas noted:

> The views about ancient India now held by scholars are based upon an examination of the Veda and the Vedic literature, to the neglect of the Puranic and the epic tradition; that is, ancient Indian history has been fashioned out of compositions, which are purely religious and priestly, ... The extraordinary nature of such history may be perceived, if it were suggested that European history should be constructed merely out of theological literature. (Pargiter 1922: p v)

The main contributor to this absurd situation—apart from the ignorance of a scientific approach to problems—was an obsession with linguistics as a historical tool on the part of nineteenth century scholars like Max Müller. This fixation led them to conclude that the history found (or imagined) in the *Rigveda* must be older than the accounts found in the Puranas because the *language* of the Vedas is more archaic.

The reason behind this archaism is not hard to fathom: the Vedas contain sacred literature that has been preserved in pristine form through the special effort of countless generations of Vedic priests and priestly families. The Puranas on the other hand have been frequently edited and modified to reflect changes in language and usage. They have also been updated to incorporate new material about later kings and dynasties. The few references to rulers that we do find in the Vedas are largely incidental. But linguists in their single minded obsession with their own theories were blind to all this. They implicitly assumed that older language necessarily meant that the contents must also refer to earlier episodes despite the fact the Vedas contain few episodes relating to history.

The illogic of the approach is revealed in its true light when we apply to English literature the same principle—of equating the linguistic age with the historical age of episodes. The English of Shakespeare's *Richard III* is undeniably older than the language of Gibbon's *Decline and Fall of the Roman Empire.* We cannot for this reason conclude that King Richard of England came before the Roman Caesars. Yet this is the yardstick used by linguists in creating their version of ancient history for over a century. It is hardly surprising that their theories should have proven so disastrously wrong when subjected to scientific analysis.

One consequence of this exercise rooted in European politics and scientific ignorance has been to confound a historical problem of monumental importance with pseudo-scientific race theories. The first and the real problem relates to the origin and distribution of languages: to wit, why people from India and Sri Lanka to England and Ireland speak languages clearly related to one another. The second, combined with half-baked linguistic ideas gave birth to the Aryan invasion myth. It is time now to disentangle the two and learn more about our ancestors, the speakers of the great Indo-European family of languages. Once we break loose from this nineteenth century strait jacket, what we have to gain is a window on a very ancient world indeed—a world before the dawn of civilizations. We have memories of this primordial world preserved in ancient Indian records—the Vedas and the Puranas, especially the latter. This also helps us find an answer to the puzzle of the origin and spread of Indo-European languages.

(This is assuming the Indo-European family of languages to have a common origin, which I doubt. I have other views on the subject that I touched in the previous chapter. We must recognize that linguistics have a major job on their hands to reformulate their theories so they don't contradict the findings of archaeology, ecology and above all genetics.)

First a few words about the sources. For historical purposes, ancient Indian sources can be divided into three types of literature—Vedic, Puranic and the historical epic. Vedic literature does not contain much history; as we have already seen it was a great fallacy on the part of nineteenth century scholarship to believe that they could find in the *Rigveda* a record of history, especially of their pet fantasy of the Aryan invasion. The result was a massive misinterpretation of the Vedas, distorting it to somehow turn it into a record of an invading Aryan race. This can be compared to turning a philosophic work like Kant's *Critique of Pure Reason* into a historical record of a Chinese invasion of Europe. To discover ancient history we must look to a different source. (This is not to suggest that the Vedas are unimportant as a historical source but only we cannot focus on them to the exclusion of the Puranic literature.)

The ancient Indian historical tradition is found not so much in the Vedas as in the epics and the Puranas. And none of these—the Vedas, the Puranas or the epics—show no knowledge of any invasion, and know of no homeland but India. They regard countries outside the borders of India as foreign lands exactly as we do today. For this reason they were rejected as unreliable for failing to support their pet theory. And a new myth was perpetuated that ancient Indians had no historical sense. This is again a charge not borne out by facts. Ancient Greeks and Chinese travelers who came into contact with India spoke respectfully of the preservation of history and traditions by the Indians. This rejection of valuable ancient records by nineteenth century scholars should be attributed to their lack of scientific training as well as prejudice. As we have already seen, most of them were missionaries and bureaucrats with axes to grind.

Once we get away from this approach, it is possible to get a remarkably coherent picture of the ancient world going back almost to the last Ice Age. But this requires not only the use of Indian records, but also the correlation of technical data from a wide variety of sources to arrive at important ancient dates. This can be based on scientific evidence, as we shall next see.

First we need to establish a chronological marker for the very ancient past. Indian tradition has always taken 3102 BC as the date when the Kali Age began, heralded by the famous Mahabharata War. Until recently, most modern scholars (including myself) had treated this date as a myth. Now more recent research—especially the unfolding ecological picture—shows that the date is in all probability close to being correct; at least there are no rational grounds for its rejection. (See Appendix II on the date of the Mahabharata War.) The strongest evidence of all comes from what we now know about the Sarasvati River and the date of the Sutra literature. Let me illustrate the idea and also the approach followed by looking at this date.

Ancient world and the birth of mathematics

The key pointer I take in establishing chronological markers is the origin of ancient mathematics, especially geometry. Mathematics has several advantages.[1] First, it has a built in logic that allows us to track the origin and growth of ideas. For instance, it is easy to see that knowledge of arithmetic must have come before algebra, and for similar reasons, calculus must have followed progress in algebra and geometry. Further, unlike language and literature, mathematical results are not affected by political and cultural biases. This is particularly relevant to the study of ancient archaeology and literature. We have seen that the Harappan sites of the Indus Valley show knowledge of town planning. This assumes knowledge of geometry.

The world had to wait more than two thousand years, until the rise of the Roman Empire before town planning and sanitation could reach the same standards as in Harappan cities. Then we also have a harbor at Lothal dating back at least to 2500 BC; it shows extraordinary engineering skill. It is the oldest scientifically designed harbor in the world (Rao 1991). There are many such examples. Clearly, such engineering feats are impossible without some knowledge of mathematics especially geometry.

Many historians have claimed that Indians got their knowledge of geometry from the Greeks after Alexander. Such claims are the result of scientific ignorance, and an unwillingness to face facts that run against long held beliefs. Harappan cities were designed and built two thousand years before Pythagoras. Even the so-called Theorem of Pythagoras (about right-angled triangles) was stated by the Vedic sage Baudhayana at least two thousand years before him. In any event we find applications of the theorem in Harappan archaeology. They could not wait for the Greeks to bring them the necessary knowledge of geometry.

The next question: where did these people get their knowledge of mathematics from? This is easy to answer. After the completion and the organization of the Vedas into its four-fold division, there came the class of literature known as the Sutras. The Sutras codified and stored all useful knowledge in the form of easy to remember mnemonic strings called 'sutras'; the word sutra in fact is Sanskrit for string. Those familiar with computing will immediately recognize its kinship to ideas in computer science. In fact, modern computer scientists are among the most serious students of the Sutra literature, especially of a great Sutra work on grammar called *Ashtadhyayi* by Panini, by common consent the greatest linguist that ever lived.

---

[1]To some it has a disadvantage also—one has to know some mathematics.

What is of interest to us here is that the Sutra literature includes the famous *Sulbasutras,* which are texts on geometry and mathematics. As I also previously noted, these *Sulbasutras* contain detailed mathematical instructions for the design and construction of Vedic altars found at various Harappan sites going back to 3000 BC. Town planning and architecture came about as secular applications of this originally religious and ritual oriented mathematics.

This in a way can be compared to the evolution of printing. The first books printed were Bibles—like the Gutenberg Bible—but the craft of printing soon went beyond its original application leading to the printing and publication of books of all kinds. And this brought about the knowledge revolution that we now call the European Renaissance. Just as the Renaissance was made possible by the printing technology initially used for printing the Gutenberg Bible, the great urban civilization of the Harappans was a secular offshoot of the religious mathematics of the *Sulbasutras*.[2]

It is helpful therefore to get some understanding of the *Sulbasutras* without actually going into its mathematical details. Bibhutibhushan Datta, who made a comprehensive study of the *Sulbasutras* observed:

> The *Sulbas,* or as they are commonly known at present amongst oriental scholars, the *Sulba-sutras,* are manuals for the construction of altars ... necessary in connexion with the sacrifices of the Vedic Hindus. ...
>
> It was primarily in connexion with the construction of the sacrificial altars of proper size and shape that the problems of geometry and also of arithmetic and algebra presented themselves, and were studied in ancient India, just as the study of astronomy is known to have begun and developed out of the necessity for fixing the proper time for the sacrifice. At any rate, from the *Sulba-sutras,* we get a glimpse of the knowledge of geometry that the Vedic Hindus had. Incidentally, they furnish us with a few other subjects of much mathematical interest. (B.B. Datta 1932: pp 1-2)

The importance Datta's pioneering work was largely ignored because most Indologists and historians lacked the scientific knowledge needed to follow it. They continued to trace Indian mathematics to Greek sources. But a careful study of the Sulbas shows that they must have been used in

---

[2]It could also be the other way, with priests using secular knowledge in designing altars. There was probably an exchange of knowledge and methods between the priestly class and others as we have today. We can only say that the oldest mathematical records are found in the Sulbas.

the design of structures, including altars, found as part of Harappan ruins. This is supplemented by the more recent work of the American mathematician Seidenberg who showed that Egypt and Babylon had borrowed their mathematics from the Sulbas. The pioneering work of Datta and Seidenberg allows us to approach a crucial date of the Vedic (and Harappan) Age on scientific grounds.

Before we approach this mathematical evidence, we may note that the authors of several Sutra works treat the Mahabharata War as ancient. The famous Sutra author Ashvalayana refers to the 'ancient sages' of the *Mahabharata* like Jaimini and Vaishampayana. Panini also refers to the *Mahabharata* and its characters like Krishna (Vaasudeva), Arjuna and others. Since Harappan archaeology presupposes knowledge of the mathematics found in the Sutra works, we can definitely say that the Mahabharata War must have taken place before the Harappan Civilization reached its peak. The Harappan cities were at the height of their glory in the centuries around 2600 BC. So the traditional date of 3102 BC is seen to be in agreement with the evidence of the Sutra literature, which mention the War.

What is significant is that the date of the Sulbasutras, which are part of the Sutra literature, is in agreement with a good deal of data from Egyptian and Old-Babylonian mathematics. This is because both Egyptian and Babylonian mathematics are based on the *Sulbasutras*. This was the discovery of the American mathematician and historian of science, the late A. Seidenberg. In fact, Seidenberg reached the scientifically epoch making conclusion:

> ... the elements of ancient geometry found in Egypt [c. 2100-1800 BC] and Babylonia [c. 1900-1750 BC] stem from a ritual system of the kind observed in the *Sulbasutras*. (Seidenberg 1962: p 515)

This means that the mathematics of the *Sulbasutras* was known to the Egyptians of the Middle Kingdom by 2000 BC. I have also shown in my own work that the construction of Egyptian pyramids going back to 2700 BC and earlier make use of ideas found in the *Sulbasutra* of Baudhayana—one of the earliest Sutra authors. Astronomy also supports the date of around 3100 BC date for the Mahabharata War. All of this cannot be just coincidence. And this constitutes overwhelming evidence for the traditional date for the War. So we can safely use this date as the benchmark.

At the same time it should be noted that this is only a date that serves as a divide between the largely spiritual age of the Vedas and the Brahmanas, and rise of the great material civilization of the Harappa-Sutra period. Whether the Mahabharata War actually took place in 3102 BC or not is not crucial for our purposes. It is only important to note that the great material age of the Harappan Civilization began about that time. On presently available evidence the date of the War can be placed between 3200 BC and 3000 BC. Any greater precision at this time is conjectural. All we need is an approximate date as a marker. Thus there is no harm in using the traditional Kali Date of 3102 BC for that purpose.

It remains only to comment upon the fact that European linguists and their modern Indian followers continue to date the Sutra literature to 500 BC or later, that is, more than 2000 years after their applications found in archaeology. The use of a little common sense will show why this is impossible. We now live in the computer age. We also have a lot of literature on computers and computing. This is because applications of computing and literature on computing have to evolve side by side. We cannot have computer applications today and computer literature coming into existence 2000 years into the future! But this is exactly what the current version of history asks us to believe. These historians are telling us in effect that while applications of mathematics can be found in Harappan archaeology c. 3000–2000 BC, the Sutra literature that forms the technological basis for the civilization was composed only after 500 BC! Only a scientific illiterate would make or accept such an argument. The Harappan Civilization and the *Sulbasutras* both belong to the Sutra period.

The roots of the fallacy of placing the literature 2000 years after their applications in archaeology lie in Max Müller's assignment of 1200 BC for the *Rigveda*. Based on this he assigned 600–200 BC for the Sutra period. Since the foundation of his chronology—1200 BC for the *Rigveda*—has collapsed as a result of science and the Sarasvati ecology, his date for the Sutra literature period built upon this foundation cannot be sustained. We have seen that Max Müller missed the date of the *Rigveda* by something like 2500 years or more. It is natural that the same error was carried over into his date for the Sutras. This is not surprising. When the foundation collapses, inevitably, the whole structure collapses.

To return to the *Mahabharata* period, it marked the end of an epoch and closed the Vedic Age. From this date it is possible to get a handle on the date of the Vedic Age that is entirely in agreement with the date derived earlier on the basis of ecology and metallurgy. Vyasa, the author of the original *Mahabharata* is equally famous for his organization and codification of the Vedas that we have today. This as we have just seen must have taken place about 3100 BC. We know from ancient geneological lists that Arjuna's son Abhimanyu who was killed in the Mahabharata War was thirty-first in descent from King Sudas of the Battle of Ten Kings fame; Sudas's priest Vasishta we have already met. Taking twenty years per generation which is known to be a reasonable average when long dynasties are involved, we get about 3720 BC for Sudas and therefore also for Vasistha. This we may recall is also the scientifically determined date for Vasistha's Head. Earlier, we noted that the introduction of silver that came after the *Rigveda* must have taken place around 3500 BC. So, the closing of the Rigvedic Age (which came with Vasistha and Visvamitra of the fourth and the third *mandalas*) may reasonably be placed between 3800 and 3700 BC.

This is also in agreement with astronomical evidence. As far back as 1893, Bal Gangadhar Tilak in India and Hermann Jacobi in Germany, working independently of each other showed that astronomical data in the seventh book of the *Rigveda* (attributed to Vasistha) points to about the same date. As we already saw, the latest data on the course of the Sarasvati River, which Vasistha describes as flowing "from the mountain to the sea" also points to the same date. We have also seen that a careful analysis of data from the French satellite SPOT (and Indian satellites later) shows that the geography and hydrology of North India described in the *Rigveda* belongs to several centuries before 3000 BC.

Therefore, on the basis of evidence from mathematics, astronomy, archaeology, ecology and metallurgy, we may safely conclude that the Rigvedic Age had ended by 3700 BC. (This date happens to be conservative; some dynastic lists lead to about 4300 BC for the Battle of Ten Kings.) The scientific evidence for this date or earlier is just overwhelming. So, nineteenth century theologians and colonial scholars (and their modern Indian followers) missed the date of the *Rigveda* by more than 2500 years! This must surely rank as one of the great intellectual blunders in the history of scholarship. But judging from what formed the foundation of their work—Biblical superstitions and linguistic speculation—the magnitude of their error is far from surprising. This is what happens when superstition and prejudice are allowed to intrude upon research. Thanks to science and more enlightened researchers, we no longer have to depend on their work.

For a summary of the findings, readers are directed to the Chronological Table given in an earlier chapter, which is reproduced below for convenience.

Period	**Dates**	**Remarks**
Great Drought	2200-1900 BC	End of the ancient world
Sarasvati river end	2200-2000 BC?	Complete drying up of the Sarasvati river
Sutra-Harappa period	c. 3000-2000 BC	Age of the *Sulbasutras*
Sarasvati civilization	Before 3200 BC	Flourishing Sarasvati river
Introduction of silver, Kunal-discoveries	c. 3500 BC or earlier	The late Veda Brahmana period
Battle of Ten Kings: seventh and the third mandalas of the *Rigveda*	3750 BC	End of the Rigvedic Age Age of Vasistha and Viswamitra
End of the last Ice Age	c. 8000 BC	Origins of the Vedic Age?

Chronological table: Ice age to the Great Drought (Ignoring the Dryases)

8.

Birth of writing: The Indus script

Indus seals and their decipherment

First a few words about the famous Harappan (or Indus) seals. We already saw that sites belonging to the Harappan Civilization were discovered by Indian and British archaeologists beginning about 1921. Among the more intriguing finds are some 4000 seals found at these sites, notably Harappa, Mohenjo-Daro, Lothal and Kalibangan. These are the famous 'Harappan seals' (or Indus seals). They contain both pictures and written messages, and have been objects of intensive study by scholars for over seventy years. The decipherment of the script and the language of the seals had remained one of the great, unsolved problems of our time, until the Vedic scholar and paleographer Natwar Jha achieved what appears to be a major breakthrough. I had the good fortune of collaborating with him on the book *The Deciphered Indus Script.*

Twilight of the Vedic Age

Before we begin to look at the script and some readings, we may summarize our major findings so far in the following statements. First, both the Rigvedic and the Harappan civilizations owed their existence to the Sarasvati River. In effect, Harappan archaeology represents the material remains of the culture and civilization described in the Vedic literature. The Harappans were Vedic Harappans belonging to the later phase of the Vedic civilization. What ended the Harappans was the complete drying up of the Sarasvati River in the 2200–1900 BC period. That is to say, the Harappans represent the twilight of the Vedic Age.

The main lesson in all this is that we cannot arbitrarily separate archaeology and literature, both coming from the same region, and attribute them to different people like the Vedic Aryans and the Dravidian Harappans. Note that archaeological sites belonging to the Harappan Civilization are found in the geographical area described in the Vedic literature. It is unnatural to separate them by coming up with an imagined event like the Aryan invasion.

This kind of separating archaeology and literature, both from the same regions, leaves us with an archaeology without literature for the Harappans and a literature without archaeology for the Harappans. This is all the more absurd when we see that Harappans had writing while the Vedic Aryans are said to have been illiterate, using only their memory for preserving their vast literature. And yet it is literature of the 'illiterate' Aryans that has come down to us while the literate Harappans seem to have vanished without a literary trace.

When we drop this absurd idea of separating archaeology and literature via a fantasized invasion, we find that there exist deep connections between Harappan archaeology and the Vedic literature. Taking just such an approach, that Harappans were also Vedic people, the great Vedic scholar Natwar Jha achieved one of the great breakthroughs of the twentieth century by deciphering the famous and enigmatic Indus script (or the Harappan script). This is the script used by the Harappans in recording their messages found on thousands of seals and other artifacts that they have left behind. Reading them enhances our understanding of the Harappans and their culture, without in any way changing the picture we obtain from other sources, including other aspects of Harappan archaeology including Vedic symbols like the swastika and the om sign that we already discussed.

The point of all this: when Harappan archaeology is replete with Vedic symbolism, it goes against all logic to assume that the language of Harappan writing is anything but Vedic Sanskrit or something closely related to it. It makes no sense to attribute an imaginary non-Vedic language to Harappan writing, but this is exactly what some, notably Asko Parpola have done.

The Indus script and its decipherment

Ever since written seals were discovered at Harappa and Mohenjo Daro, reading the script in which the inscriptions are written in has remained a major challenge. The script is known as the Harappan or the Indus script. I will be using both terms—Indus and Harappan—to designate it so it is well for the reader to know that the two refer to the same script. (Some scholars believe it should be called the Sarasvati script, but the name has not stuck. I feel it only adds to the confusion.)

One of the most dramatic developments of the final decade of the twentieth century was the decipherment of the Indus script (or the Harappan script). It was mainly the work of Dr. Natwar Jha, assisted by Dr. Birendra Kumar Jha. It marks a watershed in the study of ancient history. By a stroke of good fortune I happened to be involved in the effort, which allowed me to confirm and build on Jha's work. I was also the first to apply Jha's methodology (with some extensions) and produce a large number of independent readings. This led eventually to our book *The Deciphered Indus Script* (2000) devoted to the decipherment and interpretation of the seals.

In addition, a recently discovered example of pre-Harappan writing (discussed later), dated to c. 3500 BC, contains a reference to the *Rigveda*. This confirms two things. First, the *Rigveda* came before 3500 BC; and secondly, even in the pre-Harappan period, the *Rigveda* was ancient. This is an important development that I will discuss in more detail later. But before we can take a look at the nature of the script and what the readings have to say, an important point needs to be emphasized. Jha made the logical assumption that the language of Harappan inscriptions had to be Vedic.

Harappan language and script

It is important to see the decipherment and the subsequent work in the same spirit as what was described in the previous chapter: it links Harappan archaeology and the Vedic literature. The decipherment is by no means an isolated technical advance.

The decipherment and the readings are still controversial though several eminent scholars have accepted it. But this is only to be expected. It usually takes at least a generation for a major breakthrough to be understood, let alone verified and confirmed. I was in the fortunate position of having anticipated Jha's conclusion that the language had to be Vedic Sanskrit because of my independent finding based on Vedic mathematics and what I have earlier called the Harappa-Sutra-Sumeria connection. Once we recognize this, a vast body of literature—the Upanishads, the Sutras and much of the later Vedic literature becomes relevant in understanding and interpreting Harappan archaeology.

A point to note is that a major hurdle in deciphering the writing was the Aryan invasion theory. Advocates of this theory insisted and still insist that Harappan language can only be Dravidian and cannot be related

Sanskrit in any way. So, according to them, it is not enough to read the Harappan script; they must be read so that the results agree with their belief. For example, here is the passage from Murray Emeneau (cited earlier) expressing this dogma:

> This [Aryan invasion] is our linguistic doctrine, which has been held now for more than a century and a half. There seems to be no reason to distrust the arguments for it, in spite of the traditional Hindu ignorance of any such invasion...

This is like a believer in the Flat Earth theory insisting that a photo of the earth taken from outer space must be rejected because it shows the earth to be round, not flat. Such people can never be convinced, no matter how much evidence stares them in the face.

N. Jha with his book on the decipherment

It was precisely this wrongheaded stubbornness that held back the decipherment for more than half a century. Jha, and I later, made progress only because we rejected their theory as unfounded dogma. The Harappan script and its inscriptions cannot be read unless we acknowledge the obvious: *the Harappan civilization was Vedic, therefore its language also must have been related to Vedic Sanskrit.* For over seventy years, the decipherment of the Indus script had resisted all efforts by scholars because they refused to acknowledge this obvious fact.[1]

Jha's decipherment breaks this logjam. In a slim volume of sixty pages titled *Vedic Glossary on Indus Seals,* Natwar Jha has provided both the key to the ancient script as well as a large number of readings. After a careful examination of his work, I found his decipherment to be substantially correct. In addition, I was able to add to Jha's breakthrough by reading hundreds of seals. Jha and I were supported by many scholars, though understandably several expressed reservations also.

Further study following that announcement has only strengthened our belief about the script and its decipherment. They yield uniformly consistent readings (in Vedic Sanskrit) showing that the Harappan civilization was part of the Vedic. In addition, we can find references in Vedic and Vedantic texts for nearly all our deciphered readings. Thus there can be no doubt at all that Jha's decipherment is correct in essentials though there are bound to be questions on matters of detail.

Most important of all, the deciphered readings fit neatly into the unified historical and archaeological context of Harappan archaeology and the later Vedic literature. There is no need to concoct imaginary invasions, migrations and sudden appearance and disappearance of languages.

The decipherment confirms the findings reported in earlier chapters in almost every detail. This is not surprising because our approach was based on scientific analysis of primary evidence, not some preconceived theories. The language of the seals is Vedic Sanskrit—same as the language of the later Vedic period, which was our earlier determination also, even before reading the script. Remarkably, some of the seals contain terms given in the *Sulbasutras.* This provides direct confirmation of my own research relating the mathematics of the Sulbas to Harappan archaeology. Thus, thanks to the decipherment, we now have direct evidence supporting nearly all the conclusions reached earlier on the basis of Harappan archaeology, Vedic mathematics, as well as Sethna's comparison of Indian and Sumerian records.

It is obviously a major development that needs many years of dedicated study. The subject is necessarily technical, but it is important for any serious student of ancient history to gain at least some understanding

[1]Most of the data needed to decipher the Indus script and establish the Vedic nature of the Harappan civilization has been available for over 50 years. What held it back was the dogmatic attachment to the Aryan-Dravidian theory.

of the decipherment and its implications for history. We are not asking that every reader should accept every reading we have as correct but only that one should decide for oneself whether it makes historical and literary sense.

What I will do in the rest of the chapter is provide a brief summary of the decipherment including a few interesting readings. It appears in a book of this nature for the first time. The methodology and details with a large number of readings can be found in the book *Deciphered Indus Script* (Jha and Rajaram, 2000).

Previous efforts

After studying Jha's decipherment, and my own readings following the breakthrough, it is possible to see where previous attempts had gone astray. The first problem was that many previous scholars had rested their faith on unproven conjectures. They had taken the Aryan invasion theory, and the resulting Aryan-Dravidian linguistic divide not as theories but as proven historical facts. They thought they would find support for their theories in the Harappan seals and writings. In effect, instead of analyzing the script and the language on their merits, they had sought support in the seals (and the writing) for their own beliefs.

Technically also one can see that using any form of Proto Dravidian or any other hypothetical language was doomed to failure. *It is an impossible task trying to read an unknown script using a non-existent language.* It is best to ignore such theories and start with an open mind..

Another weakness of many of these attempted decipherments was insufficient attention to paleography, or the study of the structure of the script. A detailed study of ancient scripts is needed to grasp the basis of Indus writing. In particular, a very careful comparison had to be made with both Indian and West Asian scripts in assigning sounds to symbols. Upon such a study, what one finds is that the Indus writing was not as developed as modern Indian scripts, but was more developed than its contemporaries in Mesopotamia and Egypt. It was already showing features that would lead to a full-fledged alphabetical system like the Brahmi script used in Ashoka's inscriptions.

Above all, as Jha observed, the Harappan script is an early, more primitive form of Brahmi. Brahmi is the script used in Ashoka's famous inscriptions. It is the mother of all Indian and Southeast Asian scripts. The Indus script is the grandmother.

An additional difficulty is that in deciphering the Indus script one runs against the prevailing scholarly opinion on the evolution of alphabetical writing. Next to the Indus script, the oldest known Indian script is the Brahmi script used in Ashoka's inscriptions. Some books claim that the Brahmi script was derived from a West Asian script called Aramaic in about 700 BC. But we now know that the Indus script evolved into the Brahmi almost a thousand years earlier. In fact we find examples of writing in western India dating to about 1500 BC, displaying a transition stage from the Indus to the Brahmi.

Aramaic and Phoenician are often claimed to be the original scripts from which both Indian and European srtipts evolved. But Jha's decipherment shows that some of the features that we associate with Aramaic and Phoenician were present in the Indus script a thousand years earlier. So, if anything, Aramiac and Phoenician must have borrowed from the Indus script because the Indus is a thousand years older. Thus a radical reorientation was needed before the Indus script could be deciphered.

Steps towards decipherment

In his approach to the decipherment, Jha's first important step was to recognize the Aryan invasion and the Aryan-Dravidan divide to be modern theories that lack any support. Jha also saw that the so-called Dravidian languages like Tamil and Kannada had never existed independently of Sanskrit. Linguists have constructed hypothetical 'Proto Dravidian' languages, but these are entirely theoretical; there is no evidence that they ever existed. No one has seen a single word of this Proto Dravidian, though we have thousands of texts in other ancient languages like Pali, Prakrit, Paisaci and many others. It is strange that only this Proto Dravidan should have disappeared without a trace.[2]

Then there is another problem. According to the Aryan invasion theory, the Harappans were driven south by the invading Aryans and took their Dravidian language with them. It is strange then that they should not have taken also their script. When Dravidian languages like Tamil came to be written about 2000 years ago, they used the Brahmi script! The British when they came to India brought both their language and script, but the Dravidians took their language and not the script! It is best to disregard

[2]It might be relevant to point out that I am a Dravidian myself and both speak and write in such a language. So no one can accuse me of being a North Indian (Aryan) chauvinist opposed to Dravidians as has been done in the case of Jha.

these old theories as unfounded and focus on the data instead. It was this break from the past that allowed the Indus script to be read.[3]

Once we discard these various theories as unfounded, we are led naturally to ancient Sanskrit of the Vedic period. Jha, a Vedic scholar himself, decided to search for Vedic words on the seals. In this he was helped by an ancient work known as the *Nighantu.* It is a concise glossary of key Vedic words compiled by the ancient sage Yaska. Jha also found that the *Shanti Parva* of the epic *Mahabharata* preserves an account of Yaska's search for still older 'buried' glossaries in compiling his own glossary. From this he concluded that some of the seals must contain words found in Yaska's *Nirukta,* which is a commentary on the *Nighantu.* This gave him the clue to the language—that it must be a very old form of Sanskrit—same as the language of the *Nirukta.* This also drastically reduces the search for words, since one can limit oneself to the list of words given in the *Nighantu* instead of searching through the whole of the Vedic literature.

This can be understood by comparing Jha's approach to Jean-Francois Champollion's decipherment of Egyptian pictorial script known as 'hieroglyphics' done in the 1820s. Champollion was helped by a bilingual inscription written in Greek and Egyptian known as the 'Rosetta Stone'. In a like manner, Jha has used the *Nighantu* as the key in his decipherment. The *Nighantu* provided him with the key to its vocabulary. The two together yielded the decipherment. (This is an oversimplification, but it gets too technical if one tries to get into details.)

Since we already know the language to be Vedic Sanskrit, there was no need for a bilingual inscription like the Rosetta Stone. Where the *Nighantu* helps is in giving us a vocabulary so that we don't need to search far and wide for words appearing on the seals. Though there are words on the seals that are not found in the Vedic glossary (*Nighantu*), these too can now be read because we have the decipherment. The basic point is that two sources were needed to solve for the two unknowns—the script and the vocabulary. But the language had to be known. It had to be a real language—Vedic Sanskrit—not some imaginary one like "proto something" that never existed.

---

[3]Some recent work suggests that South Indian Brahmi scripts used in c.500 BC to write Tamil and in Sri Lanka are descended from the Indus script and not from Ashokan Brahmi. This suggests that the Indus script had at least two branches—northern and southern. This raises questions though about the accepted date of Ashoka and the Mauryas.

We may next take a brief look at the Indus writing including some examples.

Indus writing

The Indus script is one of the more complex writing systems devised by the human mind. It represents the transition stage from the complex pictorial-cum-phonetic writing characteristic of early civilizations to the phonetically precise Brahmi alphabet, which is the foundation of all Indian and Southeast Asian writing. Jha has made a plausible case that even West Asiatic scripts like Aramaic and Phoenician derive ultimately from the Indus, though this requires further study.

All of us know that modern alphabets basically have two classes of letters called consonants and vowels. (We can ignore semi-vowels; they are artifacts that most languages can do without.) Consonants represent the sounds or the phonetics, while vowels give shape to the sounds. This is how writing is done in modern alphabetical systems. But the Indus script, like most ancient scripts was *syllabic* and did not have vowels. In such a script, a word consists of a string of consonants. It is the responsibility of the reader to supply the vowels necessary to complete the word.

For example, the word 'book' would be written as 'bk', 'background' as 'bckgrnd' and so on. In fact this is how they are written in ancient scripts including the Indus script. This is called *syllabic writing*. A reader familiar with the language normally experiences little difficulty in supplying the necessary vowels and complete the word. The Indus writing is essentially syllabic with a few features found in modern Indian alphabets also. (This is an oversimplification, but will do here.)

Since syllabic writing lacks vowels it is often possible to come up with more than one 'correct' reading for the same string of symbols by superimposing different vowels. This is a feature not only of the ancient Indus script, but also the Linear B script used for the Mycaenean Greek a thousand years later, and even modern languages like Hebrew and Arabic. As a result, knowledge of the context has an important bearing on the interpretation of the signs. For instance, the examples given below have at least two different 'correct' readings depending on the vowels we choose. This is how the Indus script has to be read. The choice of one over the other is governed by the context. (I have given the English transcription for the Sanskrit letters in question. All these are taken from the seals and represent real deciphered examples.)

Letter string	**Possible readings**
s-m	saama, soma, or suma
h-m	hema, homa, or hima
bh-r-t	bharata or bhaarati
p-r-v	purva, purava, or paurava
d-sh-h-m	dasha-hema or dasha-homa
n-r-t-t-m	narottama

As a result, the context is important for a correct reading of the Indus script. This probably requires a little explanation. Someone who knows English can read Italian without understanding it. Similarly, one who can read Hindi can also read Marathi and Sanskrit without understanding much simply because they are all written in the Devanagari script and have the same sound values. *This is not possible with a syllabic script like the Indus.* One *must* know the language to read its writing.

Fortunately there is a way out of the difficulty posed by multiple readings due to lack of symbols for vowel. Although most Indus seal inscriptions are short, there are longer inscriptions also. These however do not allow so many different readings. As a result, long inscriptions can be used to check if the decipherment is correct or if it makes any sense either linguistically or in the literary context. Given below are modern transcriptions of some relatively long inscriptions with their deciphered readings.

h-r-d-r h-m-t t-v-sh-r	haridraa homaat tuvishree
a-h-v-r-n t-v s-h m-t	ahi varna tuvi sahaa mati
m-dh-dh v-g r-g v-dh-sh-v s-h-s-r dh	madvaidha raaga vedhashvai sahasradhaa

The third example is from the famous 'Dholavira signboard' found at Dholavira—a Harappan site in the Rann of Kutch. It means: "We defeated avaricious horse stealing enemies a thousand times." It might have been a victory memorial or possibly a warning sign to raiders.

Indus script is a hybrid proto-alphabet

A syllabic script is adequate as long as words in the language do not begin with a vowel. With the languages of West Asia words in them never began with a vowel, so they never had a pressing need for them. It is still the case that Arabic and Hebrew newspapers are for the most part printed without vowels. This apparently presents no problems to its readers. But Sanskrit—like English—is different. It has a high proportion of words that begin with vowels—words like *agni, indra, ishvara* and many more. To meet this need the Indus scribes had devised an ingenious method: *they used a U-shaped symbol for all vowels coming at the beginning of the word.* In the rest of the word the writing is syllabic with the reader requred to supply the vowel. (It included also a rudimentary stroke system for indicating proper vowel endings, which is not discussed here.)

With this innovation, it becomes possible to write words with vowel beginnings also. The word 'agni' is written as *Ugn.* Similarly, 'ishvara' becomes *Ushvr,* 'indra' *Undr,* 'arkagni' *Urkgn* and so on. Someone familiar with the language finds little difficulty in reading it, but the reader *must* know both the language and the literary context.

This single vowel symbol later came to be expanded to include the eleven vowels used in modern Indian scripts. The rudimentary stroke system also was perfected making the Indian writing phonetically the most precise in the world. We may therefore say that the Indus script was not as developed as modern scripts, but was more developed than its contemporary scripts in Egypt and Mesopotamia.

What this means is that the Indus alphabet is not a true alphabet but a hybrid proto-alphabet: *it is a syllabic system enhanced with a generic vowel symbol for words beginning in a vowel.*

Recognizing this fact—that it is a syllabic script with a single symbol for all the vowels—holds the key to Jha's decipherment. In addition, composite letters—a striking feature of all Indian scripts—appear also in the Indus. All in all Indus writing may be seen as an intermediate stage in the transition from a primitive consonantal system to a scientific phonetic alphabet like Brahmi from which all Indian scripts are derived.

In his book Jha gives both a complete alphabet and a methodology that anyone can use, provided the user is familiar with the language and vocabulary of the Vedic literature. It is obviously beyond the scope of the present book to go into the details of this extraordinarily rich script. What has been presented in this section is only a glimpse into the Harappan writing, describing some of its key features.

For instance, the messages on two famous seals—with the image of the bull, and the image of the horned deity or Pashupati—can now be read.

The first simply reads 'Indrah' refering to the Vedic God Indra associated with the bull as the symbol of strength. The Pashupati seal reads *'ishaadyattah maaraah'* which means: 'Maaraah (or evil adversaries) controlled by Isha'. A later section contains several examples.

Indus script as the 'missing link'

In summary, Jha's decipherment tells us that the language of the seals is Vedic Sanskrit, while the writing itself is proto-alphabetical, representing an intermediate stage in the evolution from a primitive consonantal (syllabic) system to the scientific alphabetical writing, which is the unique achievement of the Indian civilization.

The Indus script may therefore be seen as the 'missing link' between a primitive alphabet and a scientifically precise alphabet in the evolution of writing. It changes not only the history of writing but also the history of civilization itself. The veil of darkness that hid the past from us has finally been lifted. We can now say, following the sage of the *Brihadaranyaka Upanishad: tamaso ma jyotirgamaya* ("Lead us from darkness to light.")

Examples[4]

We may next look at several examples of Harappan inscriptions along with their deciphered readings. Even readers not especially proficient in Sanskrit will have little difficulty recognizing the language to be related to Sanskrit. Actually, it is Vedic Sanskrit of the post *Rigveda* period.

inah suretah

shānta (or shānti)

[4]There is considerable simplification in this chapter. I have for the most part left out the composite signs and also pictorial symbols.

attā vrisnni-sah

arka shruti

akshāgni tuvisha

dhi dhatte svargah

dāta vesha sudarshakah

deva rūpa

dvijo vāk

agnih

vāɒvagha vodha

arka-homa tri-tattvah

trāṇe indrāśvah

urṇitāshvah

arkesha-shrī yagnadru

iśādyatta mārah

These examples are from various sites including Mohenjo-Daro, Harappa, Lothal and Kalibangan, with deciphered readings. Note that language is Vedic Sanskrit but later than the *Rigveda.* The first and the last seal show a yogi seated in the *mula-bandha asana.* This shows that the Harappans practiced *yoga.* There are many examples seals and icons showing various yogic postures (*asanas*).

A pre-Harappan example: Reference to the Rigveda

Most of the seals come from what are called the mature Harappan sites like Harappa and Mohenjo-Daro and others, which have been dated roughly 2700–2100 BC, give or take a century on either side. Since the *Rigveda* is pre-Harappan, going back centuries before 3000 BC, it would be interesting if we could find and decipher some inscription from before 3000 BC or a pre-Harappan. One such example is known, which was brought to my attention in 1999. Its discoverer Richard Meadow dated it to c. 3500 BC. (There is no way of directly confirming the date, but the writing is more primitive than the bulk of the Harappan examples.

This very early example, possibly pre-Harappan may in fact go back to the period when the Sarasvati was still flowing and the Sarasvati-Drishadvati doab was the "most sacred place on earth." This solitary find (see figure below), which mentions the river by its Vedic name *Ila* and links it directly the third *mandala* (book) of the *Rigveda* serves only to whet our appetite, making us hunger for more such examples. This is discussed in some detail elsewhere, but here is the story in brief.

Example of pre-Harappan writing: It can be read as iḷāvartate vara. The reference is to a mantra in the third book of the Rigveda.

The message upon decipherment yields the reading *ilāvartate vara*—or 'ila' 'avartate' 'vara'. This is expressed in the concise *sutra* form that is the hallmark of most Harappan messages: it means 'Ila (Sarasvati) surrounds the best or the most blessed land (vara)'. This may be inferred as follows. In the *Rigveda,* Ila is another name for the Sarasvati River. (See, *ila sarasvati mahi, RV* I.14.9; *bharati ile sarasvati... RV* I.188.10.)

The deciphered message is therefore a reference to the sacred Vedic land bounded by the Sarasvati and the Drishadvati rivers. (The *Rigveda* calls it 'Ilavarta' among others.) This is clear from the celebrated Rigvedic mantra III.23.4:

> *ni tvā dadhe varā ā prthivyā ilayāspade sudinatve ahnām;*
> *dṛṣadvatyām mānuṣā apayāyām sarasvatyā recadagne didīhi.*

It is worth noting that the verse refers to the place as 'vara' meaning best or most blessed. With *ila* and *vara* appearing in both the deciphered message and the verse in question, there is little room for ambiguity: the message and the mantra above are linked.

This remarkable inscription may contain a historical reference also. It could refer to the ancient country Ilavrita mentioned in the *Mahabharata.* Its ruler was a king by the same name (Ilavrita), who received it as a gift from his father Agnidru. Ilavrita—or *ilā āvṛta*—also means 'surrounded by Ila'. So the decipherment of the 'oldest writing' is significant not only technically, but also historically. It shows that it has connection with the *Rigveda,* the world's oldest scripture and literature.

We have found several readings containing readings touching on the geography of the Vedic land. They also give an idea of the ecological pressures that the area was subject to, with references to floods as well as droughts. One of the more interesting findings is that the mighty Sarasvati, so prominent in the *Rigveda,* rarely finds mention indicating that the river was no longer mighty though there are references to the lands once sanctified by it.

In summary it can be said that the Harappan inscriptions deciphered so far confirm our other basic findings: first, the Harappans were Vedic people, and secondly, the *Rigveda* is much earlier. It may fairly said that with the discovery of Harappan inscriptions, the written phase of Indian history begins though the Vedas and the Puranas preserve a good deal of earlier accounts passed down from generation to generation both by oral tradition and in written documents that have perished.

9.

Beyond invasion: Looking south and east

The elusive Harappan horse

On the basis of the data and the explanations presented so far, we may safely conclude that various theories like the Aryan invasion theory that seek to find a home for the Vedic Aryans and their civilization outside India run into a welter of scientific and literary contradictions. Further, the roots of this version of history—one that makes Eurasia or Europe (or Afghanistan)—the original home of the Aryans are to be found in colonial politics and Christian missionary interests rather than in science or the primary sources. Nonetheless, there remain vested political and academic interests that for various reasons wish to preserve this defunct version in one form or another. It is worth looking at some of these and examine where they lead us.

Albert Einstein once said: "A theory must not contradict empirical facts." He was speaking in the context of science, especially how historians of science often lacked proper understanding of the scientific process. As he saw it the problem was: "Nearly all historians of science are philologists [linguists] and do not comprehend what physicists were aiming at, how they thought and wrestled with these problems."

When such is the situation in physics where problems are clear-cut, it is not surprising to see issues in a subject like history being much more contentious. This is particularly the case when trying to understand the records of people far removed from us in time like the creators of the Vedic and Harappan civilizations. As a result of some recent historical developments like European colonization and Western interest in Sanskrit language and linguistics, several myths and conjectures, through the force of repetition, have come to acquire the status of historical facts.

When we come to these myths, none is more persistent than the one about "No horse at Harappa." This has now been supplemented by another claim that the spoke-wheel was unknown to the Harappans. The point of these claims is that without the horse and the spoke-wheel the Harappans were militarily vulnerable to the invading Aryan hordes who moved on speedy, horse-drawn chariots with spoke-wheels. These claims are not supported by facts: an examination of the evidence shows that both the spoke-wheel and the horse were widely used by the Harappans. (The idea seems to be borrowed from the destruction of Native American civilizations by the Spanish and Portuguese 'Conquistadors'. The Conquistadors though never used chariots.)

As far as the spoke-wheel is concerned, B.B. Lal, former Director General of the Archaeological Survey of India records finding terracotta wheels at various Harappan sites. In his words: "The painted lines [spokes] converge at the central hub, and thus leave no doubt about their representing the spokes of the wheel. ...another example is reproduced from Kalibangan, a well-known Harappan site in Rajasthan, in which too the painted lines converge at the hub. ...two examples from Banawali [another Harappan site], in which the spokes are not painted but are shown in *low relief.*" (*The Sarasvati Keeps Flowing,* Aryan Books, Delhi, pages 72-3). It is also worth noting that the depiction of the spoke-wheel is common on Harappan seals. It in fact represents the letter *dha* in the Harappan script.

(The reader may find it useful at this point to go back and look at some seal reproductions in the last chapter. A few of them contain the spoke-wheel in the writings: for example the second.)

There is widespread misconception that the absence of the horse at Harappan sites shows that horses were unknown in India until the invading Aryans brought them. Such 'argument by absence' can be hazardous. To take an example, the bull is quite common on the seals, but the cow is never represented. We cannot from this conclude that the Harappans raised bulls but were ignorant of the cow. In any event, depictions of the horse are known at Harappan sites, though rare. It is possible that there was some kind of religious taboo that prevented the Harappans from using cows and horses in their art.

More fundamentally, it is simply not true that horses were unknown to the Harappans. The recently released encyclopedia *The Dawn of Indian Civilization,* Volume 1, Part 1 observes (pages 344-5) archaeologist S.P. Gupta writes: "... the horse was widely domesticated and used in India during the third millennium BC over most of the area covered by the Indus-

Sarasvati [or Harappan] Civilization. Archaeologically this is most significant since the evidence is widespread and not isolated."

This is not the full story. Sir John Marshall, Director General of the Archaeological Survey when Harappa and Mohenjo-Daro were being excavated, recorded the presence of what he called the 'Mohenjo-daro horse'. Giving salient measurements, comparing it to other known specimens, he wrote:

> It will be seen that there is a considerable degree of similarity between these various examples, and it is probable the Anau horse, the Mohenjo-daro horse, and the example of *Equus caballus* of the Zoological Survey of India, are all of the type of the 'Indian country bred', a small breed of horse, the Anau horse being slightly smaller than the others." (*Mohenjo-Daro and the Indus Civilization,* volume II, page 654.)

This is much stronger evidence than mere artifacts, which are artists' reproductions and not anatomical specimens that can be subjected to scientific examination.

Actually, the Harappans not only knew the horse, the whole issue of the 'Harappan horse' is irrelevant. In order to prove that the Vedas are of foreign origin, (and the horse came from Central Asia) one must produce positive evidence: *it should be possible to show that the horse described in the* Rigveda *was brought from Central Asia.* The *Rigveda* makes this impossible. In verse I.162.18, the *Rigveda* describes the horse as having 34 ribs (17 pairs); *while the Central Asian horse has 18 pairs (36) of ribs.* We find a similar description in the *Yajurveda* also.

This means that the horse described in the Vedas is the native Indian breed (with 34 ribs) and not the Central Asian variety. Fossil remains of *Equus Sivalensis* (the 'Siwalik horse') in India show that the 34-ribbed horse has been known in India going back to untold antiquity. This makes the whole argument based on "No horse at Harappa" irrelevant. *The Vedic horse is a native Indian breed and not the Central Asian horse.* As a result, far from supporting any Aryan invasion, the horse evidence furnishes one of its strongest refutations. Anyone arguing otherwise is beating a dead horse—literally and figuratively.

It is best to not waste more time on these straw arguments and move on to real evidence, and see where it can lead us. This is what I propose to do next.

Looking south and east

Although modern supporters of the Aryan invasion (or migration) try to justify their arguments in linguistic and cultural terms, its racial origins are always lurking in the background. There have even been attempts to connect the Indian caste system to the Aryan invasion claiming that upper caste Hindus are genetically closer to West Europeans than lower caste Hindus. This is unscientific that borders on fabrication. I have discussed the genetic evidence in some detail in a previous chapter, which demolishes all such claims.

A scientifically more acceptable explanation is that the observed physical differences among Indians are the result of adaptation to the environment by natural selection. This takes tens of thousands of years and not centuries or millennia. All this suggests that the Indian population is very ancient and not the result of any recent migrations or invasions.

There is now a new dimension to this scenario. In recent years, scholars have begun to reexamine many assumptions of the colonial period, looking in particular at the physical and biological imprint in the region. Throughout history, going back untold millennia, India's ties with East Asia and Southeast Asia have been much closer than that with Central Asia or Europe. This was interrupted by three centuries of European colonialism in the region, leading to a Eurocentric version of history being imposed on it. (The Aryan Invasion Theory was a key part of this.)

This reexamination has to begin with the recognition that Indian climate as well as flora and fauna are closely related to those of Southeast Asia. In particular, Indian cattle (*Bos Indicus*) are domesticated versions related to the wild cattle of Southeast Asia known as the *Banteng* (*Bos Banteng* or *Bos Javanicus*). Similarly, the Indian horse is a special breed, close to an ancient equid known as *Equus Sivalensis* (the 'Siwalik Horse'). This or its close relative appears to be the horse described in the *Rigveda*—and not the Central Asian or the Eurasian variety, which is anatomically different. (We just saw that the *Rigveda* describes the horse as having thirty-four ribs like the *Sivalensis,* while Central Asian breeds have thirty-six.)

It is a similar story when we examine the human imprint on the region, especially the genetic evidence. Genetic studies show that the Indian population is very ancient to which the contribution of Eurasian strains is negligible to non-existent. It is a different story when we compare Indian and Southeast Asian populations.

The overall genetic picture indicates a *very old* biological relationship, probably extending in part *at least to the original migration out of Africa.* The current understanding is that Africa was the original home of the entire human population now distributed all over the world. The overall genetic picture of Indians is that they are closely related to the Southeast Asians, going back tens of thousands of years. In contrast, their links to Eurasia or Europe find no scientific support. As a result, one thing may safely be asserted: *Indians are ancient inhabitants of India and Southeast Asia (or Greater India) and not recent immigrants.*

Maritime background

From all this it is safe to conclude that in order to understand the origins of the Vedic civilization, and its history, it is necessary first to drop the west-northwest bias that has dominated discourse for nearly two centuries. One of the keys to this is recognizing the maritime background of Vedic civilization. We have already seen that the *Rigveda* is preeminently an Indian document. While there are occasional references to the lands beyond the Indus, these are greatly exceeded by references to oceans and maritime activity. Prayers for the safety of ships and navigators occur in many parts of the *Rigveda.* This again shows a southern rather than a northwestern orientation.

Recognizing this will allow us to break free of the shackles of the northwest, particularly the Aryan Invasion Theory, which has been a major obstacle to a rational study of India. *The next logical step is to explore links between the Vedic Civilization and movements from the south, and the resulting exchanges of people and ideas between different regions.* Ecological changes, notably the ending of the last Ice Age contributed to it in a major way, in the form of two momentous developments. First, rising sea levels led inhabitants of the coastal regions, and also from now submerged regions, to move to the interior and the north seeking safer ground. Next, the melting of ice caps in the north resulted in the release of the rivers of the northern plains—making this formerly arid region fertile and inhabitable.

These two epochal events are encapsulated in the two most significant myths of ancient India—the Flood Myth of Manu and the Indra-Vritra

Myth. The *Rigveda* appears to be the product of the mix of two groups of people: tribes and ruling families that inhabited the north and poets and sages from the coastal regions and the south—some possibly from beyond the seas—who brought with them their maritime memories and experiences. This explains why the *Rigveda,* though compiled in the Sarasvati heartland, hundreds of miles from the sea, abounds in oceanic symbolism and maritime activity. But soon the distinction between the northern rulers and the southern sages came to be blurred as the two groups became intermixed.

It is no accident that two of the most important seer families of the *Rigveda*—the Vasishthas (and the brother Agastya) and the Bhrigus—should have strong maritime connections. It is important also to know that the south or the peninsular India and beyond was not unknown to the Vedic people, especially the seer families. But much information about it has been overlooked or misread in attempts to make data fit the northwestern orientation of scholars over the better part of two centuries. The main point is that in studying the Vedas, science demands that we pay much greater attention to the south and the southeast than has been the case so far. This calls for a radical reorientation.

Southern contribution

Recognizing the southern contribution to the Vedic civilization helps clarify several literary, linguistic and historical puzzles in the ancient texts. It is inconceivable that these poets and sages, who brought with them the oceanic imagery and the maritime experiences that pervade the *Rigveda* did not also bring linguistic elements and spiritual ideas that went into the Vedic language and literature. It is clear that many ancient peoples and even places have been grossly misidentified in attempts to fit history and geography to the idea of an 'expansion of Aryans' from the northwest to the south and southeast.

For example, the *Ramayana* has been misinterpreted as the expansion of the Aryan civilization into the peninsula. In reality, what Rama found in the south, even in Lanka, was a Vedic civilization. The *Uttarakanda* of the *Ramayana* is a goldmine of information about the southern, largely maritime people known as the 'Rakshasa'. The river Narmada appears to have served as the boundary between the 'spheres of influence' of the Rakshasas of the south and Ikshvakus and Bharatas of the north, with the Yadus somewhere in between. And the Rakshasa leaders often retreated to

Rasatala—the 'nether lands' (or 'Down Under')—when threatened. This *Rasatala* was probably part of Indonesia or some other region of Monsoon Asia.

What we have in all this no 'expansion of Aryans from the northwest and the north', but a free exchange of people and ideas among different regions—much as it has existed throughout history including today. And this included lands beyond the oceans. It was interrupted during the period European domination of the region. Naturally enough, they looked at history and culture of the region through Eurocentric glasses, connecting Indian history and culture to regions closer to their own. This is the 'history' that is still being followed by most establishment Indologists, especially in the West, though it is giving way under the impact of archaeology and a more rational approach to the study of the primary literature.

In summary, bringing this southern focus to ancient India appears to resolve many of the puzzles and paradoxes that plague current theories that try to explain the Vedic and Harappan Civilizations in terms of invasions and/or migrations. This is not to suggest that a southern origin for the growth of the Vedic Civilization should replace the current version. All that is being suggested is that it is an important but sadly neglected area that merits serious study. Of one thing we can be certain: trying to explain the origin and growth of the Vedic Civilization in terms of migrations/invasions a few thousand years ago runs into formidable scientific and literary obstacles. We should learn from this experience and first build a solid foundation that makes use of all data available today. Only then can we hope to recover the history of that hoary age based on the records they left behind. As Albert Einstein said: "A theory must not contradict empirical facts."

Epilogue

'History is always written wrong'

The scene before us

After this detailed, but not exhaustive look at the history of India as told by the records left by its own people, it is time perhaps to look beyond what we know and try to see what more science can tell us. This is the major task facing all of us seeking to understand more about our origins. But first it is helpful to step back and take a look at the scene unfolding before us, for the search has by no means ended. It has just begun. When we do so, what we find in most history books is little more than a jumble of mismatches—made up of mismatches between data and theories. The Aryan invasion is only the most glaring of them. In brief, here is what we find.

Contradictions galore

When we examine the accounts of ancient India as given in history books still in use, against the background of empirical data and the primary (literary) sources, what we find are fundamental mismatches between data and historical theories. These mismatches are both qualitative and quantitative in nature. Qualitatively speaking, we may note the following:

1. There is no archaeological record of any invasion and/or massive migration from Eurasia in the Vedic period. If anything we find traces of movement in the opposite direction—to West Asia and even Europe going back to the last Ice Age.
2. The geography described in the *Rigveda* corresponds to North India in the fourth millennium BC and earlier and not of Europe or Eurasia, with the Sarasvati and the Drishadvati flowing in courses where there are no major rivers today.
3. The flora and fauna described in the Vedic literature, especially those found in the sacred symbols, are tropical and subtropical varieties and not from the temperate climate or the steppes—the

supposed home of the Aryans. The *ashvattha* tree, the most sacred, is emphatically not from Europe or the Eurasian steppes. The same holds for the animals.

4. The climate described in the *Rigveda,* emphasizing the monsoon and its gods like Indra and Varuna, corresponds to that found in North India and not Eurasia or Central Asia.
5. The poetry is of a people intimately familiar with the ocean and great rivers, not of a landlocked arid region with sparse rain and insignificant rivers like in Central Asia or Eurasia. (I have discussed it in detail earlier and holds one of the keys to understanding the Vedic origins.)

In quantitative terms, there is huge time gap—exceeding a thousand years—between the dates assigned to significant features and what we actually find. These include:

1. Indian writing is supposed to be based on borrowings from the Phoenicians and/or Aramaic, but the Indus (Harappan) writing is more than a thousand years older than the oldest West Asian examples known.
2. Naturalistic art with realistic depictions is supposed to have been brought to India by the Greeks, but we find superb realistic depictions in Harappan remains. To paraphrase John Marshall, the excavator of Harappa and Mohenjo Daro: "The Indus artist anticipated the Greek artist by more than 2000 years."
3. Indian astronomy is claimed to be a borrowing from the Greeks, but the *Vedanga Jyotisha* cannot be dated later than the 14th century BC. The name itself, *Vedanga Jyotisha* indicates it is later than the Vedas. (There cannot be Vedanga without the Veda.) So the astronomical references in the Vedas must be older.
4. Migrations: The major migration or invasion is supposed to have taken place after 2000 BC, but the genetic evidence shows that the people of India have lived where they are for tens of thousands of years.

It is clear that we need a serious re-examination of history—both of the chronology and the descriptive accounts. Two fundamental tasks suggest themselves: (1) establishing independent chronological markers that connect literary accounts and datable physical features; and (2) determining the identity of the people of India on scientific grounds, independent of historical and/or linguistic theories.

In short, when we pick up almost any book on Indian history, what we have in our hands is little more than a catalog of mismatches. How do we correct this? I suggest we begin by identifying the Indian people on a scientific basis.

The Indian people

Indian literary records are the most extensive in the ancient world. Indian archaeologists have also found many important settlements going back to prehistoric times. They include not only well-known Harappan and pre-Harappan sites in India and Pakistan, but also Neolithic and Paleolithic sites, as well as cave dwellings like those at Bhimbetka in Central India. These are now being supplemented by underwater discoveries like the ones at Poompahar in Tamil Nadu and off the coast of Gujarat. In spite this profusion of records, a basic question remains: who are the people that created all this? This remains a closed chapter, if we depend soley on accounts in today's history books.

It is not as if Indian records are silent about them. We have references to various peoples like the Purus, the Turvashas, the Druhyus, the Yadus and others who remain unidentified in archaeological terms. In still broader terms, although there are many theories about their languages and culture, the Aryans and the inhabitants of the south have not been archaeologically delineated. Various historical theories make arbitrary assumptions and then use these to define important kingdoms, events, and even chronology. This is a highly unsatisfactory situation. What are needed are objective methods that lead us to chronological and historical identification of the different people of India and their contribution—in archaeology and in literature.

This identification has to address two basic issues—chronological and descriptive. We need to find objective ways of correlating the archaeological dates with the dates found in the literature. For example, if the Harappan sites in a particular region can be assigned to a particular period—say 3000 to 2000 BC—we need to find references in the literature that refer to this period. We may begin by noting that this corresponds to what is known as the Krittika period (equinox in Pleiades in Taurus). So references to this in the literature, found for example in the *Yajurveda* and the *Shatapatha Brahmana,* may be taken as the first step in establishing a chronological link between archaeology and literature.

When we come to the identity of the inhabitants, the problem becomes qualitatively different and at once more challenging. First we need to ask a basic question: are the inhabitants of India primarily of indigenous origin or are they the result of successive migrations? Various historical theories that have dominated textbooks for over a century lean towards the latter view, especially as regards the creators of the Vedic civilization. The latest edition of the *Encyclopedia Britannica* states, without citing any evidence:

> "The peoples of India are largely the product of successive invasions that have swept into the country from time immemorial. The main ethnic strains that have mingled in various combinations are the Caucasoid, Mongoloid, Australoid, and Negroid." (Volume 6, page 285)

This is purely a racist description created by colonial anthropologists, which, as I described in an earlier chapter, has been thoroughly discredited by science. This was also Karl Marx's view. It has persisted only because of his great influence on influential Indian historians even though Marx knew nothing about India. Of late, there is a tendency to attribute even the Harappan civilization to foreign inspiration, notably from West Asia and Elam. The languages of India, the two main classifications—Aryan and Dravidian—are said to be imports. The first from some "Aryan or Indo European homeland" (or Urheimat), and the latter from Scythia. I already showed how this is baseless.

From this catalog of mismatches compiled over a period lasting the better part of two centuries, it is clear that a complete overhaul is necessary. Small changes like tweaking the terminology—changing invasion to migration or influx—will not do. It simply substitutes a new falsehood for an old one. A situation like this calls for a drastic remedy. Here is what a great philosopher of history George Santayana said:

"History is always written wrong, it needs always to be rewritten."

The question therefore is not if we should rewrite history, but how. A good place to start would be to look to science and the primary sources. What I have done in this book is make a modest beginning in that direction. It is for others to decide if it is worth following upon.

Supplement I

The current state of Aryan theories

On science, history and politics

At this point, the reader might find it useful useful to have in one place a summary of the current state of affairs relating to the controversy surrounding the Aryan invasion theory and related topics. The present Supplement provides such a summary by pulling together the key facts discussed throughout the book. It gives also an account of some unexpected new developments.[1]

It is a fact of life that the idea of the Aryan invasion, tentatively put forward by some linguists in the nineteenth century came to dominate the historical discourse on ancient India. While the evidence casting doubt on the theory has been accumulating for nearly a century, residual inertia and entrenched academic interests have combined to keep the theory alive under various guises—like the Aryan migration, and, more recently, the Aryan influx.

This phenomenon of an entrenched establishment clinging to an old, discredited idea in the face of conflicting evidence is not unknown in academia, even in science. Scientists from Galileo to Einstein have had to face fierce resistance for overturning old beliefs. It is hardly surprising that scholars in 'soft' subjects like history and linguistics should be engaged in a struggle to keep alive their cherished ideas against the onslaught of science and reason. This however is beginning to change—thanks to some unusual developments in unexpected quarters.

Two seemingly unrelated developments—one in California and the other in Great Britain—will probably go a long way towards writing the obituary of the Aryan theories, and give them their long overdue burial.

[1]There is some overlap with material covered in the text, but the Supplement pulls together the relevant material in one place against the background of two recent developments: California School Board's questioning of Aryan theories and British admission that it was created to serve imperial interests.

In a manner that was proper and fitting for this largely political theory, what seems to have driven this was a political development. It took the form of a political battle involving Michael Witzel—almost the last of the Aryan theorists—and, of all things, the California Department of Education.

It is unnecessary to go into details beyond noting that Witzel's last ditch attempt to save his Aryan theories began in November 2005 when the California State Board of Education accepted the recommendations of a Commission to revise its school curriculum to reflect recent findings in history and science that demolished the Aryan invasion.

It was at this point that Witzel, a Harvard linguist, jumped into the fray uninvited and wrote a stern letter charging that the proposed revisions went against the consensus world experts (mainly himself) and if accepted would "lead without fail to an international educational scandal if they [the recommended curriculum changes] are accepted by the California's State Board of Education."

At first Witzel's initiative received attention and even deference due to a person holding a position at a prestigious place like Harvard, with his letters written on the imposing Harvard official letterhead.[2] But soon some members of the California Commission began to sense that he had a personal agenda consisting of shoring up a crumbling academic position. Scientists in particular saw his last minute interference as a gratuitous attempt to use the Harvard name (and Harvard stationery) to impress and even intimidate them.

Scientists also saw through the essential unsoundness of his theories in which the phrase Aryan invasion was used without ever defining who the so-called Aryans were. Dr. Stan Metzenberg, a biologist on the Committee appointed by the California's State Board of education said: "I've read the DNA research and there was no Aryan migration. I believe the hard evidence of DNA more than I believe historians."

This unnecessarily muddied the waters and the California Board rejected most of Witzel's changes, but tried to reach a compromise without actually throwing out all his recommendations. No matter what the final shape of the curriculum changes, it is unlikely that the Aryan theories can continue their stranglehold on history. It is only a matter of

---

[2]Witzel had also concealed the fact that ten years earlier he had to step down as Chairman of the Sanskrit Department because of scandals and threats of lawsuit. He had tried to intimidate students who spoke against his teaching and behavior.

time before this long Dark Age, dominated by dogma and politics—and political scholars from Max Müller and Macaulay to Witzel and Parpola—comes to an end. We next give a summary of the basic scientific facts.

Scientific evidence: the current state

As just observed, the California biologist Dr. Metzenberg dismissed Witzel's pretensions with the curt observation: "I've read the DNA research and there was no Aryan migration. I believe the hard evidence of DNA more than I believe historians." It is worth taking a final look at what science has to say on this and close this disgraceful chapter, even at the cost of some repetition. It essentially boils down to answering the following two questions:

1. Was the civilization of India, the Vedic civilization in particular, the result of an 'Aryan invasion' (or migration) in second millennium BC.?
2. Is there such a human group identifiable as 'Aryan'?

The answer to both these questions is an emphatic **NO.** This has been covered earlier in the book, but here is a summary.

Taking up the first question, Luigi Luca Cavalli-Sforza, Emeritus Professor at Stanford University and widely regarded as the world's foremost population geneticist, notes that the people of India, whatever their present ethnic identity, are largely of indigenous origin, going back to the Pleistocene, or the last Ice Age. The exact words used by Cavalli-Sforza and his colleagues in a recent paper are (Kivisild, et al 2004):

> ...Indian tribal and caste populations derive largely from the same genetic heritage of Pleistocene southern and western Asians and have received limited gene flow from external regions since the Holocene.

In non-technical language, this means their current genetic heritage goes back to the Ice Age (Pleistocene), or more than 50,000 years. Further, they have received limited external gene flow since the Holocene meaning they are not the result of any major invasion or migration since the Ice Age ended more than 10,000 years ago. These were discussed in some detail in the book.

This is what Dr. Metzenberg was referring to when he dismissed Witzel's claims. Similar views have been expressed by many others like the geneticist Stephen Oppenheimer of Green's College at Oxford University. *This, and not any Aryan theories, represents the scientific consensus today, no matter what Witzel, Parpola or anyone else might say.* Details may have to be changed as new evidence comes in, but one can be certain that they will not rescue their pet Aryan theories.

Next, is there an Aryan race, or, does such a thing as race, exist at all? Again, the answer of science is a resounding **NO.** Here is what Sir Julian Huxley, one of the great biologists of the twentieth century had to say as far back as 1939:

> In England and America the phrase 'Aryan race' has quite ceased to be used by writers with scientific knowledge, though it appears occasionally in political and propagandist literature.... In Germany, the idea of the 'Aryan race' received no more scientific support than in England. Nevertheless, it found able and very persistent literary advocates who made it appear very flattering to local vanity. *It therefore steadily spread, fostered by special conditions.* (Italics added.)

'Special conditions' fostered the Aryan myth

This brings us to the second recent development in the form of the British admission of the political nature of the theory. The passage cited above sheds light on two factors (shown in italics) that have kept this discredited and indefensible idea alive, especially in academia: (1) political and propagandist interests; and (2) special conditions. These 'special conditions' (as Huxley called it) led to this scholarly pathology being foisted as a central dogma of ancient historiography. These conditions grew out of nineteenth and twentieth century political currents growing out of German nationalism and British imperial needs.

As we saw earlier, the notion that Indians are one branch of a common stock of people who lived originally in Central Asia or in the Eurasian steppes arose in the late eighteenth century. It began as a linguistic theory to account for similarities between Sanskrit and classical European languages like Greek and Latin. From this modest beginning it soon acquired a life of its own when scholars, especially in Germany, concluded that Europeans and ancient Indians were two branches of a people they called Aryans and later as Indo-Europeans. A whole new academic discipline called Indo-European studies came into existence whose very survival is now at stake following scientific discoveries.

The Aryan theory, which began life as a linguistic theory soon acquired a biological form. Scholars, mostly linguists, began to talk about not just Aryan languages, but also an Aryan race. Since Indology had its greatest flowering in nineteenth century Germany, it is not surprising that racial ideas that shaped German nationalism should have found their way into scholarly discourse on India. The Indo-European hypothesis and its offshoot of the Aryan invasion (or migration) theory came to dominate this discourse for over a century.

It is important to recognize that the people who created this theory were, and are today, linguists (like Michael Witzel), not biologists. We have already seen that scientists, including German scientists, have no use for it. Its perpetuation then and its survival today is the result of 'special conditions.'

These 'special conditions' were the rise of Nazism in Germany and British imperial needs in India. While both Germany and Britain took to the idea of the Aryan race, its fate in the two countries was somewhat different. Its perversion in Germany leading eventually to Nazism and its horrors is well known and not needed here. The British, however, put it to more creative use for imperial purposes, especially as a tool in making their rule acceptable to Indians. A recent BBC report admitted as much (October 6, 2005):[3]

> It [the Aryan invasion theory] gave a historical precedent to justify the role and status of the British Raj, who could argue that they were transforming India for the better in the same way that the Aryans had done thousands of years earlier.

That is to say, the British presented themselves as a 'new and improved brand of Aryans' who were only completing the work left undone by their ancestors in the hoary past. This is how the British Prime Minister Stanley Baldwin put it in the House of Commons in 1929:

> Now, after ages, ...the two branches of the great Aryan ancestry have again been brought together by Providence... By establishing British rule in India, God said to the British, "I have brought you and the Indians together after a long separation, ...it is your duty to raise them to their own level as quickly as possible ...brothers as you are..."

---

[3]Available on the internet at http://www.bbc.co.uk/religion/religions/hinduism/history/history5.shtml

This leaves little to the imagination. As the BBC report also noted: "The theory was not just wrong, **it included unacceptably racist ideas**"

It is time to give this pathological theory a decent burial and study the records that ancient people have left behind, without labels or stereotypes like 'Aryan', 'Dravidian' or anything else. While science and history have discredited this aberration of scholarship, entrenched academic interests are still striving to keep its corpse alive. This, however, cannot go on forever. It is only a matter of time before the theory as well as its advocates both disappear, perhaps within a generation.

Supplement II

Science in Ancient India

Unfounded assumptions

One of the basic assumptions about the ancient Hindus is that they were not of a scientific bent of mind. This prejudice was created in the nineteenth century by the same people who created also the Aryan invasion model. We have already seen that even the most eminent of them, like Max Müller, lacked the rudiments of science, believing in superstions like the Biblical Creation and the story of Noah and the Flood. But as usual many Indian historians have unthinkingly accepted this as gospel truth. The prejudice of Indians as an unscientific people is so ingrained that their Indian disciples dare not even question it. Being themselves ignorant of science, they attribute the same drawback to others. It applies to them, so they assume it applies to all others.

This assumption is now discredited by archaeology and other sources. Even a cursory examination of the great cities, harbors and citadels of the Harappan Civilization show its creators to have been highly skilled city planners, engineers and architects. A closer examination reveals no less impressive mastery of metallurgy, mathematics and other sciences. But historians holding on to their outdated assumptions have ignored all this. In any event they probably lack the necessary background in science and technology to understand and interpret them.

One consequence of this prejudice—of regarding Indians as unscientific—has been the attribution of the scientific achievements of the ancient Hindus to foreign sources. An attempt was made at first to derive Indian mathematics and astronomy from the Greeks, but this proved impossible. Next attempts were made to derive them from Mesopotamia, especially Babylon. But this also creates a problem, though the problem probably lies beyond the comprehension of Indian historians steeped in scientific ignorance. In any event, here is the problem: since the

Harappan civilization had been thriving for more than a thousand years before the Old-Babylonian empire of Hammurabi (c. 1900-1750 BC), they could not have used Babylonian mathematics in designing their cities and buildings. The harbor of Lothal was designed and built around 2500 BC which rules out any Babylonian influence. They must have had their own earlier source. This source we now know to have been preserved in the *Sulbasutras*—thanks to the work of Datta and Seidenberg, and also archaeology.

What is most extraordinary in all this is the following: the charge of lack of scientific capacity on the part of Indians is made by those who are themselves scientifically ignorant—like nineteenth century European theologians and linguists continuing down to their modern Indian followers, especially Marxist historians. It is interesting to contrast their views with those of competent scientists who studied ancient India—that is to say the views of people who knew what they were talking about when it came to science. This will help shed light on the true fact—of prejudice and unfounded charges used as a fig leaf to conceal their own scientific ignorance. Here are a few examples.

Albrecht Weber was a leading nineteenth century Sanskrit scholar from Germany. At a time when the relationship between Indian and Greek mathematics was being seriously debated by historians of science, Weber went on to assert that the Sulbas were borrowed by the Indians from the Greeks following Alexander's invasion. His actual statement was that there was "nothing of a literary-historical nature standing in the way of the assumption of a use [by the Sulba authors] of the teachings of Hero of Alexandria." Hero of Alexandria is now known to have been living in 62 AD! Even in Weber's time Hero was known to be later than 200 BC (A. Weber 1884. Review of L. von Schroeder's 'Pythagoras und die Inder.' *Literarisches Zentrablatt* 35, p 1564.) Now of course we know that the mathematics of the Sulbas must have existed long before 2000 BC for the Harappans to have used them. This is clear from archaeology. And this, as we also saw, is supported by the mathematical records of Egypt and Old-Babylonia.

One more example: William Dwight Whitney was a nineteenth century American philologist. He once wrote in his book on Sanskrit grammar of all things:

> The astronomical science of the Hindus is a reflection of that of Greece, and

> its literature of fairly recent date; but as mathematicians, in arithmetic and geometry they have shown more independence. Their medical science ... is of little account ... by no means ancient.

The issue is not whether he was wrong—though he was—but that he should have thought himself qualified to express opinions on scientific subjects. The same is true of what some others said about astronomy. A.B. Keith gave out the view that Indians had borrowed their astronomy from some 'Semitic source' without specifying which one. Keith was a linguist serving as a bureaucrat in the British colonial office. He was entirely ignorant of science, but that did not stop him expressing opinions about scientific subjects for which he was wholly unqualified.

I mention these not to discredit these scholars—science has already done that—but to caution readers, especially the youth, not to accept something simply because it is stated in an authoritative manner by someone with a great reputation. Nothing should be accepted unless it is substantiated by evidence and sound reasons. Even then we must be prepared to change our views based on new facts and new evidence. Bhagawan Buddha expressed it best when he said: "Accept nothing on my authority. Think, and be a lamp unto thyself." This is the method of science. It is also the way to progress.

Let us next take a brief look at ancient Indian sciences as seen by scientists qualified to express opinions on the subject.

Expert views on ancient Indian sciences

While this has continued to be the view of people who were (and are) for the most part scientific illiterates, it is interesting to contrast their views with what scientifically qualified men had to say about ancient Indian sciences. We already saw what the late A. Seidenberg, an outstanding mathematician and historian of science (professor of mathematics at the University of California at Berkeley) had to say about the Sulba: he called it 'The Origin of Mathematics'. It is similarly illuminating to contrast Keith's statements with what Jean-Sylvain Bailly, a leading French astronomer had to say about the astronomical record of the Hindus (noted by S. Sathe in his *Search for the Year of Bharata War*. 1982. Navabharati, Hyderabad. p 32). But characteristically, European scholars and their modern Indian followers have chosen to ignore the observations of competent astronomers, just as they now are pretending that modern findings from mathematics and even archaeology make no difference. Here is what Bailly had to say:[1]

> ... the motions of the stars calculated by the Hindus before some 4500 years vary not even a single minute from the tables of Cassine and Meyer [used in Europe in the nineteenth century]. The Indian tables give the same annual variation of the moon as that discovered by Tycho Brahe—a variation unknown to the school of Alexandria and also to the Arabs who followed the calculations of the school. ... The Hindu systems of astronomy are by far the oldest and that, from which the Egyptians, Greeks, Romans and even the Jews derive the knowledge.

We shall see a little later that this receives support from Medieval Arab sources also. Another important discovery made by European astronomers studying Hindu texts is that the Kali Date of 18 February 3102 BC represents actual observations made on that day. The positions of the stars and planets given for that date agree remarkably well with the calculations made with the help of modern computers.

Some modern scholars—mostly colonial-missionary scholars and their modern Indian disciples—have tried to dismiss this finding by claiming the Kali Date to be a modern forgery arrived at by 'back calculation'. Fleet for one claimed that this back calculation was done in c. 400 AD.

But this kind of 'back calculation' calls for the use of Newton's Law of Gravitation as well as the solution of differential equations; neither of these was known in ancient times. For instance, Aryabhata or anyone else living in c. 400 AD would not have been able to calculate correct stellar and planetary positions as they existed 3500 years before him. The necessary scientific and mathematical methods just did not exist at the time. Even today, using modern computers, such 'back calculations' of planetary positions are far from easy. So the observations must have been genuine, made and recorded on 18 February 3102 BC, and preserved for posterity to this day. John Playfair, Astronomer Royal at the University of Edinburgh pointed this out. So Hindu astronomy must already have been quite sophisticated—at least from an observational point of view.

We must be prepared to recognize that preserving a few astronomical

[1]Jean-Sylvan Bailly (1736–93) died on the guillotine, a victim of the Terror that followed the French Revolution.

records was not beyond the capacity of a people who preserved such voluminous records as the Vedas and Puranas for thousands of years.

Further, the great material civilization of the Harappans would have been impossible without fairly detailed practical knowledge of astronomy. The Sarasvati (or the Harappan) civilization was spread over a million and a half square kilometers and might have supported tens of millions of people. A civilized population of that size over such a vast area presupposes knowledge of time-keeping and calendars which could only have been based on astronomy. All other methods came much later. Further, archaeology is showing that the Sarasvati-civilization was a maritime civilization as we already saw in the previous chapters. Otherwise they would not have built sophisticated harbors like Lothal. Navigation also requires knowledge of observational astronomy.

Even in the *Rigveda* we find references to seasonal navigation and migratory birds. Here is a famous *Rk* showing that the Rigvedic civilization made use of knowledge of the seasons for navigation (my translation).

> *He who knows the path of the birds flying in the sky, he knows the course of the ocean going ships.* *Rigveda I.25.7*

There are technical reasons also why the so-called 'sidereal' Hindu astronomical calendar should have come before all others. It need not detain us here. It is sufficient to know that based on these considerations, the British astronomer John Playfair estimated that Hindu astronomy must go back at least to 5000 BC; I believe it must be at least a thousand years older than that. Both David Frawley and Lokamanya Tilak have found references in the *Rigveda* that point to dates before 6000 BC. I am not claiming that the *Rigveda* is that old, only that we find astronomical references pointing to that era.

It is not only modern scholars who regard Indian science as the oldest and as the origin of all sciences. Medieval and ancient scholars from Arabia, Spain, China and even Greece acknowledged their indebtedness to Indian science. A medieval Arab scholar Sa'id ibn Ahmad al-Andalusi (1029–1070) wrote in his *Tabaqat al-'umam,* one of the earliest books on history of sciences:

> The first nation to have cultivated science is India. ... India is known for the wisdom of its people. Over many centuries, all the kings of the past have recognized the ability of the Indians in all the branches of knowledge.

> The kings of China have stated that the kings of the world are five in number and all the people of the world are their subjects. They mentioned the king of China, the king of India, the king of the Turks, the king of the Persians, and the king of the Romans.
>
> ... They referred to the king of India as the "king of wisdom" because of the Indians' careful treatment of '*ulum* [sciences] and all the branches of knowledge.
>
> The Indians, known to all nations for many centuries, are the metal [essence] of wisdom, the source of fairness and objectivity. They are people of sublime pensiveness, universal apologues, and useful and rare inventions.
>
> ... To their credit the Indians have made great strides in the study of numbers and of geometry. They have acquired immense information and reached the zenith in their knowledge of the movements of the stars [astronomy] ... After all that they have surpassed all other peoples in their knowledge of medical sciences...

When the necessary allowance is made for the exuberance of the writer and some possible exaggeration, it is clear that no one until the coming of the modern Europeans (and their Indian disciples) questioned the antiquity of Indian science. In his book al-Andalusi goes on to give details of several Indian texts on astronomy and tells us that the Arab scholars used them in preparing their own almanacs.

Not only Medieval Arabs, but also some early Christian scholars recognized Indian contributions. Writing in 662 AD, Sebokht, the Bishop of Qinnesrin in North Syria observed:

> I will omit all discussion of the science of the Hindus [Indians], a people not the same as Syrians, their subtle discoveries in the science of astronomy, *discoveries more ingenious than those of the Greeks and the Babylonians;* their valuable method of calculation [the decimal system]; their computing that surpasses description. I wish only to say that this computation is done by means of nine signs.

But ultimately, we don't need the opinions of any experts; we have abundant evidence of the scientific knowledge of the Vedic people in the cities and harbors they have left behind, metallurgical artifacts, scientific instruments, and the vast body of scientific and mathematical literature—all of which are available to anyone who wants to study them.

The point of all this: we must ignore the version of ancient Indian history found in textbooks as the creation of colonial scholars serving the Church and the Empire and their Indian Marxist disciples (serving themselves). The first step in this is to revise our idea of ancient Indian science with the help of scientifically competent scholars. We live in the age of science and technology. There is no excuse for living with incompetence based on scientific ignorance. There is no reason why we should pay heed to the opinions of scientific illiterates like nineteenth century theologians who believed in Biblical Creationism, and their modern disciples when the views of competent scholars are available. When we apply such a scientific approach, the picture of ancient India that we get is completely different from what is given in history books.

What I have described in these pages is no more than a glimpse of what science and an unprejudiced mind can uncover about the ancient past. What is given here is not the last word, but a new beginning. It is no more than the first step on our path to rediscovery. It would be worthwhile for young men and women with scientific knowledge to study ancient Indian works in the original and draw independent conclusions.

At the same time we should acknowledge that it is not just nineteenth century scholars and their modern followers, but all of us calling ourselves modern, who have been guilty—guilty at least of greatly underestimating the age of our origins. By this we have failed to appreciate that Vedic India was a primordial civilization in which change is bound to be much more gradual. They didn't have other civilizations to copy and to borrow from, as Japan had the West. Everything had to be originated from basic raw materials and human thought. Mere ingenuity and adaptation does not suffice to create a civilization where none existed before.

Such mighty creative endeavor takes not decades nor even centuries, but many millennia. The 'Greek miracle' which was achieved within a few centuries was possible only because they had earlier sources—Egypt, Babylon and India—to draw from and build upon. The same is true of the modern United States, which borrowed from Europe, and later Japan, which in turn borrowed from both. This emphatically was not true of the Vedic Civilization. It was a slow fire that simmered for several millennia until it finally burnt itself out in a brilliant blaze in the great material civilization of the Sutra-Harappa period.

Is the world now headed on a similar course—a great material civilization blazing to extinction? Will this be the end of the Kali Age as forecast by Veda Vyasa 5000 years ago? If indeed it is, we still have the *Rigveda*, the primordial source from which all knowledge sprang. The great cycle can repeat, beginning with a new Krita Yuga—the Age of Truth. The *Rigveda* will be there to guide us.

And its sages: *purvebhirishibhiridyo nutanaih*—worthy of homage, sages ancient and modern—says the *Rigveda*.

Supplement III

Date of the Mahabharata war

Background

The Mahabharata War is a watershed of first importance in the study of ancient India. Scholars have long noted that the *Mahabharata,* like a good deal of ancient literature, has numerous references to astronomical positions, which in principle can be used to date events described in the epic, including the War.

For well over a century, scholars have attempted to date the Mahabharata War using the profuse astronomical data available in the text. There are two fundamental problems associated with such astronomical data. First, the accuracy of the records, which may have been corrupted over time. Second, even when the data are accurate, whether the date refers to the date of the event (like the death of Bhisma) or the date at which the passage was composed, and possibly interpolated. Paradoxically, it is easier to filter out corrupt readings and arrive at reliable data than it is to recognize interpolated passages that give dates with data that appear to be consistent. This can be illustrated with the help of the famous record of Bhisma's death at the winter solstice (longest night or the beginning of winter).

In the *Anushasana Parva* of the *Mahabharata,* there is a famous statement according to which Bhisma lying on a bed of arrows died shortly after the onset of the winter soltice in *Magha*. On the basis of this several scholars have attempted to compute the date of his death and hence of the Mahabharata War. It is unnecessary to go into the details, but as I have shown elsewhere, it yields a date that is demonstrably impossible. The picture becomes clear once we recognize that the passage in question is a later interpolation. From this it is natural to conclude that the poet (the interpolator) must have described astronomical positions in his own time rather than at the time of the War. This is because the *Mahabharata* is the work of several hands.

Though the astronomical method of dating has for the most part enjoyed limited success, recent advances in computer software, especially of the kind known as planetorioum programs offer exciting possibilities. This has allowed some mathematicians to arrive at a reasobnable date for the Mahabharata War.

Remarkably, calculating before such software became available, the late Professor K.R. Srinivasaraghavan (known also as Raghavan) arrived at the following dates: Lunar Eclipse: 28 September 3067 BC; Solar eclipse (New moon): 13 October 3067 BC. If confirmed, it would be an interesting observation because the *Mahabharata* records them as occurring just before the Kurukshetra War. The Memphis-based astronmer Narahari Achar recently confirmed and gave more details.[1]

The basic point that Achar notes is that eclipses depend on the motions of the moon, which has a short period. Planetary positions on the other hand repeat themselves much more slowly and therefore accumulate fewer errors. In his words:

> It is regarded that planetary positions are most reliable and eclipses and comets are not so reliable. The most important planetary position for purposes of this exercise is considered to be Shani at Rohini. (Saturn at Aldeberan) This configuration has been stressed both by Karna in *Udyogaparva* and by Vyasa in *Bhishmaparva*. A solar eclipse at Jyeshtha (Antares) is considered to be the next important event. For, the new moon at Antares, has been mentioned by Krishna, and the solar eclipse has been mentioned by both Karna and Vyasa. The preceding full moon at Kartika (Pleiades) was a lunar eclipse day, again mentioned by both Karna and Vyasa. Retrograde motion of Mars before reaching Antares and the occurrence of the winter solstice in Magha Shukla Paksha complete the list of required astronomical events, the references to the original in Sanskrit can be found in the work of Sathe et. al.[2]

This has the merit of preserving also the sequence of eclipses mentioned in the text: a lunar eclipse followed by a solar eclipse. These took place in a

[1]This material has been published in the volume *Dating the Mahabharata War by Astronomical Data,* published by the Mythic Society, Bangalore. The article is available on the internct at: http://www.hindunet.org/saraswati/colloquium/narahari01.htm

[2]This was the conclusion reached by Rajaram and Frawley in *Vedic Aryans...* also though their approach was more speculative. Note the extraordinary consistency of these crucial astronomical positions spread across *two parvas* and noted by several individuals, namely, Krishna, Karna and Vyasa. This rules out any coincidence or later fabrication by 'back calculation'.

month that was particularly rich in eclipses, or what Achar calls an 'eclipse season.' Achar next describes his methodology of using different astronomical software systems to compute different aspects of the problem. (No single program can address all the problems satisfactorily.)

> A search was made using the planetarium software SkyMap Pro6, from 3500 BCE to 1000 BCE, for the years in which Saturn was in conjunction with Aldeberan. There are a hundred conjunctions in this interval. Then a search was made from among these 100 conjunction years to find the years in which there was also a solar eclipse at Antares. The planetarium software RedShift 3 was used for this purpose. It turned out that there are 11 years in which Saturn was at Aldeberan, and a solar eclipse at Antares occurred. A further search was made from among these 11 years to find those in which there was a lunar eclipse at Pleiades immediately before the solar eclipse at Antares. This reduced the set from 11 to six. These years are: 3244 BCE, 3067 BCE, 2890 BCE, 2360 BCE, 2183 BCE, and 1682 BCE. Then a search was made for those years in which Mars executed a retrograde motion before reaching Antares and became prograde again by the time the solar eclipse occurred. Out of these six, there were two years in which Mars did not execute retrograde motion and two years in which Mars became retrograde much later or in some position other than near Antares.
>
> There were only two years, 3067 BCE and 2183 BCE, in which Saturn was at Aldeberan, there was a solar eclipse at Antares, preceded by a lunar eclipse at Pleiades, and Mars had executed retrograde motion before reaching Antares. These two years could be the possible years for the Mahabharata War.

The choice for the date of the Mahabharata War therefore comes down to choosing between 3067 BC and 2183 BC. Achar settles in favor of the former based on his conclusion that the record of Bhishma's death following the winter solstice in Magha is accurate. This however forces him to accept an *adhi masa* (or *adhika masa* or intercalary month). We have already noted that this is could be an interpolation. We reject the later date (2183 BC) on archaeological grounds: by then the draught of 2200 BC–1900 BC had already set in and the Harappan civilization was well into decline. The post *Mahabharata* period however saw a good deal more activity in the creation of the Upanishads, the Brahmanas, the Sutras as well as the division of the Vedas, including the separation of the *Yajurveda*.

We may therefore choose 3067 BC as the most probable date for the Mahabharata War. This receives additional astronomical support in the mention of the Rohini-Krittika transition mentioned in the *Mahabharata,* which is impossible for the 2183 BC date. We provide additional data below that support the earlier date. It should be an object of humility to modern scholars that this date of 3067 BC was computed by K.R. Srinivasaraghavan some forty years ago, without the help of computers or astronomical software! It is one of the most amazing computational feats in modern times.

The Mahabharata tradition

The astronomical data given by the eclipse pair and planetary positions do not stand alone. We have other data from the post Samhita Vedic literature that supports the traditional date of c. 3100 BC (or 3067 BC). Ashvalayana, a very early Sutra author records:

> *prācināviti sumantu jaimini vaiśampāyana pailasūtrabhāṣya bhārata mahābhārata dharmācaryāh.* *Ashvalayana Grhyasutra,* III.4

This tells us that in Ashvalayana's time Jaimini was known as the author of a work called *Bharata* and Vaishampayana of the *Mahabharata*. This happens to agree with the account in the *Mahabharata* itself. It is interesting that Paila's name appears on at least one of the Harappan seals. The message on the seal is: *adi-sarge paila.* This means 'Paila (appears) in the first *sarga* (or part)', as indeed he does in the *Adi-parva* of the *Mahabharata*.

Ashvalayana also records that in his time plants sprouted after the beginning of monsoon rains in the Hindu month of Bhadrapada. This now takes place in Jyestha or Ashadha. This goes to show that the monsoon in his time used to start in the month of Shravana and not in Jyestha as is the case today. This is clear indication that the Hindu calendar has moved forward relative to the seasons by more than two months. This is due to a well-known astronomical phenomenon which astronomers call the 'precession of the equinoxes'. Seasons fall back relative to the fixed stars (and the Hindu calendar which is based on the fixed stars) by about one day every 72.5 years. What this means is that the beginning of monsoon noted by Ashvalayana must have been taking place close to 5000 years ago or about 3000 BC.

Ashvalayana provides another piece of information in the form of observations of the pole star. We are used to seeing the pole star Polaris in the constellation Ursa Minoris (Little Bear) marking the North Pole. But this was not the case in his time. The pole star also moves with the seasons, due the precession of the equinoxes. As a result there has not been a pole star through much of human history. The last major star to mark the North Pole was Thuban in the constellation of the Dragon. Its technical name is Alpha Draconis. The pole star observed by Ashvalayana can only have been Alpha Draconis, which again places him around 3000 BC.[1] Further, Ashvalayana pays homage to his teacher Kahola Kaushitaki who also records astronomical observations pointing to the same approximate date—that is to say, about 3000 BC.

This Kahola Kaushitaki was the sage of the *Kaushitaki Brahmana.* It mentions several *Mahabharata* characters. It also mentions that the winter solstice—as the first day of winter is called—took place on the day on which we now celebrate the Maha-Shivaratri festival. The winter solstice now falls on December 21, and the Maha-Shivaratri comes within a week of March 1. This is due to the precession of the equinoxes. And this movement as we saw takes place at the rate of one day about every 72.5 years. Since the time of the *Kaushitaki Brahmana* the seasons have moved by about 70 days. So, 70 times 72.5 or about 5100 years must have passed. This corresponds to a date of about 3100 BC. The Mahabharata War must therefore have taken place about this time. In particular we have no reason to reject the 'Raghavan date' of 3067 BC, which lies quite close to the traditional 3102 BC.

In summary we may say that the astronomical record is in general agreement with the tradition: the astronomical Kali and the historical Kali (Mahabharata War) came close together. The agreement between the computed dates and the recorded dates must be regarded quite close considering the ancient dates involved and the manner in which they were recorded, going through several hands and revisions. Further, it reconciles astronomical and other technical data from several sources that appear at first sight to be contradictory.

---

[1]By 2183 BC, Alpha Draconis had moved away from the pole; i.e., there was no pole star.

Bibliography

Original works cited

Amarakośa
Aṣṭādhyāyi (of Panini)
Baudhāyana Śulbasūtra
Mahābhārata (of Krsnadvaipayana Vyasa)
Manudharma Śāstra (Manu Samhita)
Pancavimśa Brāhmaṇa
Ramāyaṇa (of Valmiki)
Rigveda (Ṛk Samhita)
Shatapatha Brāhmaṇa
Yajurveda (Taittiriya Samhita and *Vajasaneyi Samhita)*

References

Agarwal, Ashvini, Editor. 2005. *In Search of Vedic-Harappan Relationship.* New Delhi: Aryan Books International.

al-Andalusi, Sa'id. 1991. *Science in the Medieval World: Book of the categories of nations.* Translated and edited by S.I. Salem and Alok Kumar. University of Texas. Austin, Texas.

Aurobindo, Sri. 1991. *On the Mahabharata.* Pondicherry: Sri Aurobindo Ashram.

Bhagwan Singh. 1995. *The Vedic Harappans.* New Delhi: Aditya Prakashan.

Bodmer, Walter and Robin McKie. 1994. *The Book of Man: The Quest to Discover Our Genetic Heritage.* London: Abacus, p 225.

Cavalli-Sforza, L.L and F. 1995. *The Great Human Diasporas.* Reading, MA: Addison-Wesley.

Cavalli-Sforza, L.L 2001. *Genes, Peoples and Languages.* Penguin.

Danino, Michel. 2001. *The Invasion that Never Was.* Mysore: Mira Aditi Center.

Datta, B.B. 1993. *Ancient Hindu Geometry: Science of the Sulba.* New Delhi: Cosmo.

Emeneau, Murray. 1954. Linguistic prehistory of India. *Proceedings of the American Philosophical Society,* Vol.98, pp 282-92. Philadelphia.

Francfort, Paul-Henri. 1992. Evidence for the Harappan irrigation system in Haryana and Rajasthan. *Eastern Anthropologist* 45: 87-103.

Frawley, David. 1991. *Gods, Sages and Kings.* Salt Lake City, Utah: Passage Press. (Indian edition by Motilal-Banarsidass, New Delhi)

Frawley, David. 2001. *The Rig Veda and the History of India.* New Delhi, Aditya Prakashan.

Gupta, S.P.2005. The Sarasvati and the homeland of early Rigvedic Rishis: In the light of recent scientific researches. *In Search of Vedic-Harappan Relationship,* Edited by Ashvini Agarwal. New Delhi: Aryan Books International: 55-74.

Hicks, H.H. and R.N. Anderson. 1990. Analysis of an Indo-European Vedic-Aryan Head—4th millennium BC. *Journal of Indo-European Studies* 18: 425-446.

Jha, N. 1996. *Vedic Glossary on Indus Seals.* Varanasi: Ganga-Kaveri Publishing House.

Jha, N. 1997. 'New Approach to the Study of the Indus Script and Language', edited and translated with notes and comments by N.S. Rajaram. *Quarterly Journal of the Mythic Society* LXXXVIII. 1 (January-March).

Jha, N. and N.S. Rajaram. 2000. *The Deciphered Indus Script: Methodology, Readings, Interpretation.* New Delhi, Voice of India.

Kisilvid, T. S. Rootsi, M. Metspahi, S. Mastana, K. Kaldma, J. Parik, E. Metspalu, M. Adojan, H.-V. Tolk, V. Stepanov, M. Gölge, E. Usanga, S.S. Papiha, C. CinnióIu, R. King, L. Cavalli-Sforza, P.A. Unterhill and R. Villems. 'The Genetic Heritage of the Earliest Settlers Persist Both in Indian Tribal and Caste Populations.' 2003. *American Journal of Human Genetics,* 72: pp 313-332.

J.B. Kruskal, I. Dyen and P. Black, 'The Vocabulary and Method of Reconstructing Language Trees: Innovations and Large Scale Applications' in *Mathematics in the Archaeological and Historical Sciences* (1971) edited by F.R. Hodson, D.G. Kendall, and P. Tatu, Edinburgh University Press, Edinburgh.

Le Mée, Jean, trans. 1975. *Hymns from the Rig-Veda.* New York: Alfred A. Knopf.

M. Bamshad, T. Kivisild, W.S. Watkins, M.E. Dixon, C.E. Ricker, B.B. Rao, J.M. Naidu, B.V.R. Prasad, P.G. Reddy, A. Rasanagam, et al. 'Genetic Evidence on the Origin of Indian Caste Populations.' 2001, *Genome Research* 11, pp 994-1004.

Merton, Robert K., David S. Sills, and Stephen M. Stigler. 1984. The Kelvin dictum and social science: an excursion into the history of an idea. *Journal of the History of the Behavioral Sciences* 20: 319-31.

Misra, S.S. 1992. *The Aryan Problem, a linguistic approach.* New Delhi: Munshiram Manoharlal.

Mukherji, S.N. 1987. *Sir William Jones: a study in eighteenth century British attitudes to India*. Hyderabad: Orient Longmans.

Oppenheimer, Stephen. 2003. *Out of Eden: The peopling of the world.* London: Constable.

Pargiter, F.E. 1913 (Reissued 1975). *Dynasties of the Kali Age.* Delhi: Deep Publications.

Pargiter, F.E. 1922 (Reissued 1979). *Ancient Indian Traditions.* New Delhi: Cosmo.

Radhakrishna, B.P. and S.S. Mehr, editors (1999) *Vedic Sarasvati: Evolutionary History of a Lost River in Northwest India.* Bangalore: Geological Society of India.

Rajaram, N.S. 1993. *Aryan Invasion of India: The myth and the truth.* New Delhi: Voice of India.

Rajaram, N.S. 1995. *The Politics of History: Aryan invasion theory and the subversion of scholarship.* New Delhi: Voice of India.

Rajaram, N.S. 1996. Jha's Decipherment of the Indus Script. *The Quarterly Journal of the Mythic Society* LXXXVII. 4 (October-December).

Rajaram, N.S. 2002. Sarasvati Ecology and the Vedic Civilization. *The Quarterly Journal of the Mythic Society,* Vol.XCIII, Issues 304: July-December 2002.

Rajaram, N.S. 1997. Decipherment of the Indus Script: A Personal Account. *PRAJNA*, Vol.1, number 3, July-September 1997.

Rajaram, N.S. 2004. *Search for the Historical Krishna.* Bangalore: Prism Books.

Rajaram, N.S. 2004. Population Genetics on Human Migrations. *The Quarterly Journal of the Mythic Society,* Vol.XCV, Issue 3: July-September 2004.

Rajaram, N.S. 2005. Connections between the Harappan seals and the Vedic literature. *In search of Vedic-Harappan Relationship,* edited by Ashvini Agarwal. New Delhi: Aryan Books International, pages 135-41.

Rajaram, N.S. 2006. History as An Extension of Natural History (To appear).

Rajaram, N.S. and David Frawley. 2001. *Vedic Aryans and the Origins of Civilization,* 3rd edition. New Delhi: Voice of India.

Rao, S.R. 1991. *Dawn and Devolution of the Indus Civilization.* New Delhi: Aditya Prakashan.

Renfrew, Colin. 1990 [1973]. *Before Civilization: The radiocarbon revolution and prehistoric Europe.* London: Penguin [Jonathan Cape].

Rgveda Samhita, Volume I. 1977. Sanskrit text edited and translated by Svami Satya Prakash Sarasvati and Satyakama Vidyalankar, New Delhi: Veda Pratisthana.

Sathe, S. 1991. *Aryans: Who were they?* Mysore: Bharatiya Itihasa Sankalana Samiti.

Sathe, S. 1991a. *Bharateeya Historiography,* 2nd edition. Hyderabad: Bharatiya Itihasa Sankalana Samiti.

Seidenberg, A. 1962. The Ritual Origin of Geometry. *Archive for History of Exact Sciences* 1: 488-527.

Seidenberg, A. 1978. The Origin of Mathematics. *Archive for History of Exact Sciences* 18: 301-42.

Sethna, K.D. 1981. *KARPASA in Prehistoric India: A chronological and cultural clue.* New Delhi: Biblia Impex.

Sethna, K.D. 1992. *The Problem of Aryan Origins: From an Indian point of view.* Second enlarged edition. New Delhi: Aditya Prakashan.

Shaffer, J.G. 1984. Indo-Aryan invasions: cultural myth and archaeological reality. *In* John R. Luckas, ed. *People of South Asia.* New York: Plenum.

Shourie, Arun. 1994. *Missionaries in India: Continuities, changes, dilemmas.* New Delhi: ASA.

Street-Perrott, F.A. and R.A. Perrott. 1990. Abrupt Climate Fluctuations in the Tropics: The Influence of Atlantic Ocean Circulation. *Nature* 343: 607-12.

Talageri, S. 1993. *Aryan Invasion Theory, A reappraisal.* New Delhi: Aditya Prakashan.

Talageri, S. 2000. *The Rigveda: A historical analysis.* New Delhi: Aditya Prakashan.

Varma, K.C. 1979. Editorial Note in *Age of the Bharata War,* G.C. Agarawala. New Delhi: Motilal-Banarsidas.

Weiss, H., M-A. Courty, W. Wetterstrom, F. Guichard, L. Senior, R. Meadow and A. Curnow. 1993. Genesis and collapse of third millennium North Mesopotamian civilization. *Science* 261: 995-1004.

Index